Short Stories

Anatoly (Tony) Kandiew

Order this book online at www.trafford.com
or email orders@trafford.com

Most Trafford titles are also available at major online book retailers.

Print information available on the last page.

ISBN: 978-1-4907-5460-4 (sc)
ISBN: 978-1-4907-5461-1 (e)

Trafford rev. 03/30/2015

 www.trafford.com

North America & international
toll-free: 1 888 232 4444 (USA & Canada)
fax: 812 355 4082

Contents

George of Samos

One sunny April day, I walked with Bob down Madison Avenue. Bob had become a friend of mine by association. I would select the equipment for General Reinsurance and Bob would provide me with the best leasing arrangements. Then, I would take the combined dada to our Treasurer and he would decide whether we purchased or leased. Bob was able to structure the lease so well that it was usually more advantageous for the company to lease rather than purchase. We had just attended a symposium on leases.

All of a sudden, Bob stopped dead in his tracks and exclaimed: "George, is that you?..."

I was rattled by his sudden outburst. Obviously they knew each other. We approached each other. They chatted briefly before Bob introduced me.

Then, George turned to me, "Mr. Kando, nice meeting you. Do you happen to have your resume on you?"

At first, I thought, this was kind of rash. So, I gave him my "how dare you be so blunt look." But, Bob stepped up, "Tony, it's ok. Give him your resume if you have it on you."

Somewhat reluctantly, I opened my briefcase and handed him my resume. Not that I was looking for a job. I had the best job in this world already. But, in those days I had my resume handy.

George took it, read it and, put it in his vest pocket.

Then, I heard him mumble, "NASA, eh." He turned to me, "Mr. Kando, let me give you a ride in my limo to your office. I have a brief meeting. You are welcome to attend. When we are done, I will have my chauffeur take us to Greenwich. I will get you there before this train does," as he pointed to Grand Central Station.

I saw Bob smiling from ear to ear. Something had to be "up." I kind of looked at Bob as he gave me that "go ahead" look. So, I agreed. Instantly George parted with Bob and practically ran to his office with me in hot pursuit, maybe a half step behind him.

Later I found out that George did that on purpose with every new "potential customer." As far as he was concerned, he was going to leave the impression that he was extremely busy and well organized.

This was George's second visit to America. In the first visit he came penniless, got a job with Plaid Stamps and made a fortune, more than 10 million dollars. Then, he decided to retire. He sold everything and moved back to Samos.

There, he bought himself a motorcycle and rode the breezy shore of the Mediterranean Sea. But, no sooner that he retired the Greek Government went bankrupt. All his deposited money was lost in a massive "haircut" and currency reform. So George put on his "thinking cap" and came to America to make his second fortune...

When we arrived at his office, George whizzed by the secretary. Then, he stopped abruptly. I heard him say, "Eileen, this is Mr. Kando. Please set up a seat for him. We'll be right in."

Eileen practically jumped off her chair and made a beeline towards two polished oak doors. There, she disappeared.

George walked up to the water cooler, poured a cup of cold water and offered it to me. I gulped it down. Beautiful water I thought. George noticed. Next, I heard him say "The best...From Spring Minnewaska... delivered every day!"

At that moment Eileen returned. I saw her give a 'slight nod.' George turned to me and we walked in. We barely crossed the threshold when I heard:

"Let me introduce Mr. Kando to you."

All faces stared at me, as if I had just arrived from the moon. George pointed to the seat for me, while he took center stage. And, almost nonchalantly he began a monologue: "Gentlemen, let me tell you about fleeting assets...."

As George spoke, his audience was mesmerized. I started watching the attenders, then George and then, again the attenders. I heard him talk about: "Empty Airline seats...; empty Hotel rooms...; empty Villas..." and then, I heard him say: "Idle computer time..."

This got my attention, and while he took a deep breath, I piped in: "Everybody has some idle machine time..." I barely finished, when George leaped from his seat, as if catapulted from a jet fighter. In his left hand he held my resume, and with his right hand finger he practically pierced it.

Then, he exclaimed at the top of his lungs: "Did you hear this!" And, then, in a much lower pitch: "Did you hear this! This man just put NASA on the map in America!"

And, 22 eyes turned on me, all wide open. I felt they wanted to nail me to the wall behind me. But, then I heard a collective: "Ah," as they just stared at me.

With that George handed out forms, called in Eileen and announced: "Eileen, you take care of these gentlemen. My chauffeur will take Mr. Kando and me, in my limo to his office." He came up to me, and together we left the room...

George headed for the phone. He punched a few numbers. "Are you ready?...OK"

We took the elevator to the basement. A huge, black limo waited for us. A chauffeur beckoned at the back door. George mumbled, "After you, Mr. Kando..."

When we were comfortable, he pushed a button. A bar opened.

"How about a drink?" I heard.

I nodded. "Scotch and soda... near virgin... please..."

In a jiffy the drinks were ready,

"Here's to a great afternoon... to a new friendship..."

"I second that..."

After a few sips, he said "May I call you Anatoly?"

"My friends call me Tony," I replied.

"I like that. Call me George. I like informality. To hell with all that bulle..."

He raised his glass.

"Directions please..." As I instructed George, he repeated parts to the driver. The driver tipped his hat.

"What did you think of my seminar?"

"Very interesting... I never heard anything like that. How does it work?"

"I match up fleeting assets. America overproduces. I can get you anything you want... at no cost...," he fumbled in his vest pocket. Out came a few sheets.

4

His neatly typed list was organized by product group. I was struck, the Who's Who of American business was on it: Airlines, Automobiles, etc. I paged through it, it had about 1000 vendors.

"This is only a summary. My detail list is about 200 pages," George said.

I liked his confidence. It was catchy. My department was a pure expense item. Data processing was always an expense item. Everybody complained about the cost: "All this overhead," everybody would say. With George my department might become a producer. "What a blast!" I thought.

"What kind of computer do you have?" he started.

"An IBM 158."

"How much is machine time?"

"About $5,000 an hour prime shift; $3,000 third shift."

"I'll take all the time you got for 5 years," I heard.

Wow, I thought. This was an immense deal. Say I only gave him third shift, 6 (days) X 8 (hours) or 48 hours. Times 52, roughly 2500 hours per year, not counting Sunday. Then, Sunday. Another 24 hours. Adjusted for third shift. Another 2500 hours. I had 5,000 hours at $3,000 or $15 million a year. For 5 years, that's $75 million dollars. What a bonanza!

"What about staffing?" I asked.

"How about, 5 people, $100 an hour," I heard.

That was about 17% more, or 2.5 million. My entire budget for 52 people was less than 1.5 million.

"George, what if I need back up time?"

5

"No sweat. Even swap. How's that?"

"What happens when I give you my schedule and you don't sell the time. Who eats the fleeting asset?"

"Tony, don't worry. As soon as you give me your schedule, I am responsible. If I don't sell it, I'll eat it. We have a fixed contract."

That was wonderful. But, "George, you realize I have to pitch management and then, get it past legal. You understand..."

George smiled, "Of course. But, remember this: Each day will cost you $30 grand. Each Sunday over $100 grand. It's up to you, to get your act together." We were already at our Toll Both.

"George, may I have your card. Give me a number where I can reach you after 'dark'..." I fingered for my own card and gave it to him, while George scribbled a number on his. Before I could look up, his driver had pulled into our first entrance.

I loved George's idea. This was supreme Job Security. Next, I had to find a catchy "closer." We had roughly 400 employees at the Fortress at Steamboat Road.

Suppose, I proposed that: Each employee would get a "Christmas bonus." ONE BRAND NEW CAR. Maybe, ONE BRAND NEW CAR WITH THE COMPLIMENTS OF THE DATA PROCESSING DEPARTMENT each and every year. That, would be a twist, wouldn't it? At $15,000 X 400, that was only $6 million. Times 4, $24 million.

I went straight to my office. I got a sheet of paper and played back the numbers. They were right on the money. Then, I called Mike. He was my number 2. I wanted to run it by him first. I wanted to hear his honest opinion before I would proceed. I got him seated.

As I talked his face kept dropping. He dropped his cigar and almost burned his suit. Mike was speechless. Then, "Tony, we've got to do it!"

"Mike, for now, mums the word, until I have this character checked out," Mike agreed.

"Are you going to tell Frank?" Frank was my boss.

"Of course."

As I approached Frank's office I saw him laughing in his glass "cage." (All the executive offices were glass "cages." My Operations Manager often said, "You can't even scratch yourself in private"). He waved me right in.

"I just got a call from the front desk. Please don't drive up in our Chairman's limo. They nearly had a heart attack..." as he laughed.

"Frank, I have something that's different. I have not verified everything. But, here it is..." Then, I painted the same picture to him as I did for Mike. Frank was laughing even harder.

"Tony, do you realize what you got? For once we can play offence. Until now, we were defense. How many times does the defense win a game?" he mused. Next, I added my "car closer." Now, he laughed out loud, "What do you think this is? A car welfare system? No, that won't fly. Give me your numbers, I'll run them by Tom." Frank took my notes and disappeared to represent my plan to upper management. Tom was the leading Actuary in the company.

When Frank came back he called me into his office. And, with a hearty laugh he started, "Tom loves the idea. His only concern is: Do we have the time? What if something comes up? Otherwise, you've got the green light. All systems are go..."

Peter the Great

I am not talking about the Czar who called his country Rossija, from the Dutch word Ross or horse, effectively naming it "The Land of Horses."

Voltaire was hired by Catherine II, a German adventuress, to write the first definitive Rossijan History, as directed by the Muscovite ruler and nobility. Naturally, for the right price, Voltaire obliged. And Voltaire was paid handsomely for writing what the Rossijan rulers wanted to hear. Upon completion, Voltaire sent Diderot to collect his final installment from Catherine II.

It was Voltaire who called Peter Great, for what reason? Was it because Voltaire was paid a great amount of money? What other reason could it possibly be?

Usually a ruler or king is called great when he or she accomplishes a great deed, such as the introduction of Christianity, or is a great conqueror who was never defeated in battle. Surely no conqueror was called great when he was taken prisoner by his enemy, as Peter was in the Pruth Campaign. Peter was captured and was made prisoner by the Sultan! Then, his Lithuanian sex slave had to ransom him from the Sultan. A grateful Peter later married her and she became his wife and successor. She ruled as Catherine I, for only a short while.

Certainly no conqueror who was defeated by a token force of Swedes was ever called "Great." Especially when the Swedish King was only 16 years old (Charles XII) and commanded an army of only 14,000, while Peter commanded more than 60,000 brave Rossijans. Charles defeated

Peter so badly that Peter ran as hard as he could all the way from Narva (a Baltic Seaport), to Moscow. And, when Peter arrived, he ordered all church bells to be taken down and cast into cannons. That is, he not only abandoned his army, but left all his cannons behind in great haste.

In return, Voltaire is eulogized in the Hermitage with a statue prominently displayed for all to see, and with the best library that money could buy. And, from then on, every Rossijan historian of any "salt" had to have a dedication to Voltaire in his history, presumably so that Voltaire's propaganda may be continued in perpetuity.

Voltaire was paid handsomely, but he had to promote Peter's "Greatness." This found fertile soil in the West. Thus, as one can see, deprived intellectuals will say anything if there is enough gold for them.

Voltaire called Peter's realm "Russe" in spite of Peter's choice, for Voltaire was in awe of Rus (the Ukraine or Kiyivan Rus). Before the invasion of the Tartars, the Ukraine was the largest and most powerful country in Europe. The Ukraine was the major reason why the Roman Empire (Constantinople) survived, because the Ukraine provided not only the grain but also the "muscle power" Constantinople needed. The "Praetorian guard" had long since been replaced with the "Varangian guard" from the Ukraine. Once the Ukraine was destroyed by the Tartars, Constantinople was destroyed shortly thereafter.

Actually, it was Ryk or Rik and not RUS. The original spelling is PYC in Greek or Cyrillic and is pronounced RUS if it were all Greek. But Rome had replaced the Greek traders. Thus the last two letters are Roman (explaining commonality), while the first is Greek (indicating the roots). (Anyone who worked on "name clearance" or other phonetic algorithms knows that).

Thus, the RYC spelling is easily explained this way: the first letter is Greek since they traded first in the Ukraine, while the other two letters are Roman.

In addition the first "real" Capetian King, Henry I, was married to Anna, the daughter of King Yaroslav, the hereditary King of Kiyivan Rus.

In addition, the Hohenstauffen line starts with the Holy Roman Emperor Henry IV and Adelaide, a Kiyivan Princess. And, Volodimir (Vladimir when russified) was crowned King by the Emperor of the Roman Empire, Basil II. Volodimir was the only King ever to marry into the house of the Roman Emperors. He married the Emperor's sister, Anna. Kiyiv was made a Patriarchate. The only legitimate Patriarchate, east of the Vistula River. (This is still a NEMESIS today in Putin's Russia).

In those days, future European monarchs stood in line to woo a Kiyivan Princess, such as: Henry of France, Harold of Norway and so on, to seek alliances and to transplant culture to their realm. At that time, Kiyiv's "Sister City" was Florence. And when the dauphin signed the marriage contract, his signature was a large X while Anna's signature was clean and meticulous. This contract is still prominently displayed for all to see in Kiyiv. Thus, in spite of Peter's choice, the present day use is "Russia" in the West, as imposed by Voltaire.

But, to this day, the fabricated writings of Voltaire are accepted as facts. Meanwhile, the present day Russians still call their country Rossija, not Russia. (See any modern postage stamp from Russia).

I am not talking about Peter who banished his wife into a nunnery, for the rest of her natural life, simply because her sexual acrobatics were inadequate for him. Eventually, Peter was gifted a teenage Latvian/Lithuanian "sex slave," who proved to be all he bargained for. She ranked at par with Aphrodite, Messalina, and Theodora. And, after she ransomed Peter from the Sultan's captivity, during the Pruth campaign, a grateful Peter made her his wife. Eventually, she ruled as Catherine I.

Of course Peter's womanizing got him the dreaded venereal disease Syphilis (on his second trip to the West, in Paris). Thus, in Rossija, Syphilis is still called the "French Disease." Peter died in agony from third stage complications. Thus, his later offsprings were truly idiots, i.e. Peter III.

I am not talking about Peter, who tortured and killed his son and heir, causing a succession crisis. It was the second major crisis in Rossija's history. The first was created by Ivan the Terrible who also killed his son and heir.

Ivan the Terrible destroyed the last Ukrainian holdout from the Tartars: Novhorod (pronounced Novgorod when russified). Novhorod had survived the Tartar conquest because it was spring and the siege engines could not be moved. So the Tartars bypassed Novhorod. Novhorod survived by joining the Hansa, a maritime federation of Swedish and German cities from about 1239 to 1580 or nearly 350 years. After Ivan conquered Novhorod he killed 50,000 burgers. Then, he proclaimed: "Now ring your liberty bell."

The rest of the population was exiled to the Ural mountains where they formed the Ural Sich (a Cossack fort). Puhachov tried to find safety in the Ural Sich, but general Suvorw captured him and brought him to Moscow for a "show trial" for Catherine II. To show you the "humanitarian" treatment: Puhachov was placed into a cage just big enough to hold him. Then, by the orders of Catherine II, he was hauled from the Urals to Moscow without ever leaving the cage. He arrived looking like "Big Foot," all overgrown hair and like a wild animal. (Does this remind you of the show trials Hitler had when he punished the von Stauffenberg conspirators.) Terrorism speaks the same language everywhere.

Then, Ivan captured Kazan, one of the Khanates of the "Golden Horde." And, again after the conquest he butchered 50,000 Tartars. When the Astrakhan Khanate heard of the butchery they surrendered without a fight. Well, Ivan went in and butchered 50,000 for good measure anyway. Thus, two of the four Khanates were destroyed. Just before Ivan died, the Tartars from the Crimea invaded Muscovy, in order to avenge Ivan's bloody sack of Kazan and Astrakhan.

This time, however, the Tartars rounded up the entire population of Muscovy. They drove them like cattle to their slave markets in the Crimea. More than one million of them! Thus, from then on, only Tartars remained in all of Muscovy. Hence, Boris Godunov took over. Hence, it can be easily said that Rossija is populated primarily by Tartars or Mongols.

Just prior to the Crimean Tartar invasion, Ermack a Hetman from the Don Sitch, with a price on his head, took a contingent of Cossacks and invaded Siberia. He defeated the Siberian Khanate and gifted the land to Ivan the Terrible, who made him governor of the province.

Thus, all of Muscovy was in Tartar hands, even the Czar was a Tartar. This, the Ukrainians could not tolerate. Thus, the Zaporozhian and Don Cossacks stepped in. They took Moscow and called a Sbor, an Allthing in the Gothic tradition (a gathering of all Gothic/Slavic people). And they came from all parts of Rus. Thus, the Cossacks elected Michael Romanov. Hence, Tartar rule was averted while the population of Muscovy remained mostly Tartar.

Needless to say, Peter was a fan and admirer of Ivan the Terrible. But, the Cossacks were vilified. The end result was that Germans ruled Rossija, starting with Catherine II.

Catherine's son, Paul, was illegitimate. He was the product of her illicit affair with her German chamberlain or a Polish Prince. Paul married a German Princess from "Hesse",(from Hanover). And, their offsprings married only German Princesses thereafter, all from "Hesse." That is, they are all related to the "House of Hannover" or Hohenstauffen). Does that ring a bell? (Queen Elizabeth II is a descendent from the House of Hannover. And recently the Prince of Wales, Charles, condemned Putin's actions in the Ukraine calling them at par with Hitler's action. Hence, from then on, the entire Romanov lineage became 100% German.

I am not talking about Peter, who is claimed to have formulated the "Table of Ranks." Leibnitz formulated the "Table of Ranks." Peter just plagiarized it. And, like every plagiarist, Peter made a few crucial mistakes. He left the German names for fear of altering Leibnitz's master list. Thus, the German words "Ober," "Unter," "Prokuror" and "Feldwebel" entered the Rossijan language.

I am not talking about Peter the great reformer, who butchered the Ukrainian language. He crossed out a few letters of the Ukrainian alphabet: "h," "i," "ï" etc. Then, he called it the Rossijan alphabet. Now, try to pronounce the word "honorarium." This sounds like a contagious disease, doesn't it?

In addition, Peter changed the calendar of seasons to the calendar of the Greco Roman gods and demigods. Thus, "Jan(us), Febr(us), Mar(s), April, May(a), Jun(o), Juli(us) (Caesar), Augustus (Caesar)" were honored in Rossija just as they were in the West. And, for the rest of the old Roman ten month calendar, the months nine and ten were left alone.

Finally, to muzzle the Orthodox Church (the only legitimate Patriarch can be only be in Kiyiv, Ukraine), Peter chose a grandiose name: The "Holy Synod" (as suggested by Leibnitz). It was made up of four lay and three cleric electors, all nominated by the "Imperator," to elect a "Metropolitan" in Moscow (the only unchartered city in RUS). Thus, from then on the Czars of Rossija ruled without any moral authority whatsoever.

Rather, I am talking about my boss's cat who was called "Peter the Great." Peter was an extraordinary cat. He loved music, not just any music, mind you, but "classical music" and "classical opera," that is, music by Beethoven, Bach, Mozart, Verdi, Wagner and so on.

My boss was called Yosh. He was the director of the Applied Math Department of a national laboratory.

Once, Josh had a visitor from Germany who worked on the "Four Color Problem." He came to the Lab to grind out a solution by "enumeration," which seemed to lurk around the corner using his method (which proved to be false). The "Four Color Problem" happens to be a problem for which every printer has a solution. Moreover, there is an analytic solution for every space and surface except for a sphere. So, practically every mathematician of name has spent at least a few years of his life trying to solve this problem. But, the solution has been elusive to this day.

That visitor, Heinrich, was also an accomplished violinist. One day, Heinrich was invited by Yosh and his wife Kimi to play his violin.

Yosh and Kimi lived near the Lab in the "hinterlands," where plenty of trees have still defied the onslaught of the bulldozers.

Peter was a domesticated cat. Yet, he loved to roam the backwoods. However, as soon as he heard classical music, he was "Johnny on the spot." He would drop everything and rush to his home. This way, Peter would not to be denied a musical treat. Peter not only loved the music, but he also judged the performers. When he did not like the music or the performer, he simply left quietly and went back to the woods. There, he pursued his sport.

When the guests arrived, Peter was gallivanting in the woods. But, as soon as Yosh put on Wagner's "Die Götterdämmerung" Peter rushed in. He seized up the guests and claimed the most prominent place among them, right in the middle of the living room. There, he made himself comfortable, with the rear curled up and the front attentive like a Sphinx. He knew a treat was in store for him.

After some small talk, Heinrich volunteered to play. And, when Heinrich played, Peter seemed to look at him in wonder. Peter was probably the most attentive spectator that evening. And, at the end, if he could have, he would have applauded... And, if he could have, he would have yelled "Brava, Brava, Brava..."

Peter was decidedly taken in by Heinrich's performance. We could see it. Peter approved...

When Heinrich finished, Peter waited, so as not to miss anything of importance. But then, he jumped up and disappeared in the woods. He returned shortly thereafter with a mouse in his fangs. Then, he approached Heinrich, and laid the dead beast at his feet!

So, this is my story about two cats; one killed for food, the other killed to satisfy his vanity.

Crownvic, Toys With Their Own Mind

Seven years ago I moved in with my mother. She could not get around any longer on her own. For the last 29 years she was getting by with her tricycle in the hinterlands. She was a truly amazing woman.

I had just finalized my divorce and planned to move West. I have a "bum" knee which disables me during cold spells. And, since Florida has no real jobs, at least not in my capacity, I was tempted to move West. I am a mathematician, specializing in system and quantitative analysis. These jobs go begging in the North East and in the West. But, not in Florida or the South. The main jobs in Florida are: Municipal, Entertainment, Mowing or plain Scams (telemarketing etc.) But, with plenty of sunshine. Therefore, I was inclined to move West. However, my mother pleaded with me to join her, which I did.

I had a small pension from one of my jobs and Social Security was just around the corner. So, I took my personal items and settled with my Ex. We kissed and parted company. I found a job in my specialty in Englewood, which turned out to be another scam. But, that's another story.

The car I owned was an Olds Cierra, vintage 1990. It was a medium size car. However, my mother had difficulty getting in and out of it. So, I was on the lookout for another car. But, this car had to be 'tailor made' for her.

I don't like new cars. It takes too long to brake them in. And, their depreciation is horrendous. While I was casually looking, one fine day my Olds developed a terrible clanking noise, a terminal malaise for any car. I took her promptly to my local repair shop, Trail Auto.

When the "chief mechanic" examined the noise, he declared that the engine was shot. Thus, the end had come with a bang and left me without wheels.

As the mechanic was pontificating his diagnosis, a customer approached me. He made me an offer: My car and some cash for an Ex Police Cruiser. A Crown Victoria, with a search light, in good running condition. The mechanic knew the car and assured me it was in good driving condition. All she needed was only a few minor repairs. They could be taken care of with $200 or so. Most importantly, the deal could be made right away.

This was too good to be true. My guardian angel must have caused this happenstance! I agreed to the deal with one stipulation: My mother needed to "stress test" the car. The seller agreed. So, we went to his home in his car and I test drove the Ex Police Cruiser. And, indeed, the car was in good running condition. The ac was ice cold. And, she drove steady as a rock: No shimmying, no fish tailing. She "purred" as she hugged the road.

We drove to my house for the acid test. I asked my mother to enter the car. And, she loved it. Thus, the deal was finalized on the spot and I became the owner of an Ex Police Cruiser.

When I called my insurance company, my rates were reduced by 20%, because the car had ABS brakes! Next day I went to the Motor Vehicle Bureau to get the title. And, more amazing tidbits...

The prior owners had disconnected a few items: The odometer, the heat, the oil gage and the battery gage. But, according the "grandfather clause," I was absolved of making them work. Instead, on my title it states in bold letters: POLICE CAR. Therefore, only the car knows for sure for how many miles it endured its riders...

My repairs ended up to be a new battery and two new tires. I tried to fix the odometer. But, my mechanic refused. He claimed this was illegal! Thus, I am left with this minor inconvenience which I don't mind at all.

Once the car was fixed, I took her for a spin to Sarasota. On that trip I had another surprise coming. As I drove up behind a car, the driver quickly moved out of my way...

It seems everybody recognizes Police Cruisers when they see one. So started my "love affair" with my Crown Victoria. I love it and my mother loved it!

Meanwhile, my Ex, called me from time to time. Sometimes to kick a few ideas around, sometimes to cry on my shoulder. I must say in all fairness, until her malaise, I never called her. Yet, she kept calling me. My mother was not particularly fond of her, until her malaise.

Thus, on one occasion when she called, I told her about my "new car." She was appalled that I bought a "boat," a disheveled jalopy. She likes Hondas and Toyotas of the same vintage. And, she refused to consider that my mother would have to turn into a "pretzel" in order to fit into those "Kinderwagens!" Thus, she developed an instant dislike for my toy. And, believe it or not, my toy disliked my Ex. Here is how.

Let me preface the incidents with the following: Except for the troubles with my Ex, my toy has NOT GIVEN ME ONE SPECK OF TROUBLE since I owned it. And, that is close to three years.

First incident. My Ex decided to open a Real Estate Office in Fort Lauderdale. She found an enchanted "Bohemian" area. There she started her business. But, in every business the first year is crucial. Needless to say, she began on a shoe string. But, with a lot of confidence in her ability to sell, and she is quite good at it. However, as things started to turn sour, she kept calling me practically every day. So, I decided to combine business and pleasure, and pay her a visit, to uplift her spirits and just maybe, to help her with her business.

Therefore, I made arrangements with my sister. She agreed to stay with my mother while I would go and do some gallivanting. The day my sister arrived, I left for Fort Lauderdale.

The ride was smooth and uneventful. But, as I approached my Ex's domain, my car started to heat up. Then, as I was within viewing distance of her office, my car "died." Two blocks away from my destination, my car just gave up. In front of a traffic light. With a huge puddle on the ground. Clearly, my car was not willing or able to move another inch. In fact, she needed to be towed and reconditioned...

Second incident. After my mother died, my Ex decided to visit me, to uplift my spirits or just to escape from New York this last December after 9/11 and, stay at my place for a month or so. She rented her New York flat (a studio for $2,600 a month). Then, using the Internet, she found a cheap flight to Fort Myers on Jet Blue. And, she was on her way. Naturally, I volunteered to pick her up.

On the appointed day I drove to the Airport. The drive there was uneventful. The return drive was fine until she started complaining about my car. And then, from out of nowhere my car started to "smoke." Thank goodness we were practically at home. But, for the last mile or so, my toy was fuming...

The upshot was: Because of my car's sensitivity, I was absolved from taking her around. Thus, my Ex used our public transportation to satisfy her needs...

Third incident. Unexpected business, forced my Ex to change her plans. She had to return to Fort Lauderdale before year's end. But, in Venice, our local "big town," there was a Christmas concert she wanted to attend. We took my car. As we approached our destination, she started to bad mouth my car for no apparent reason. Guess what? My car responded by fuming...

Eventually, we made it home safely. But, it is crystal clear that the animosity between them is "for real." She left the 27th of December 2001 and, my car has been running like a champ ever since. Since then I drove to Sarasota, to Venice, to Punta Gorda and so on. And, I had not one speck of trouble...

I welcome you to put your collective minds together and give me a rational explanation...

A Game Called Köppen

Once my "stamp business" was firmly in place the "money was rolling in" in a steady stream. Now I could divert my attention to other things while maintaining a fair balance between school and my business.

At the end of the war there was a general state of idleness as Berlin was mustering her energies to rebuild. But, youthful energies need an outlet, and the first manifestation was the formation of STREET GANGS. It was "macho" to belong to your street gang. So, I joined our street gang also. Street gangs are exceptionally well organized. Our's had a GENERAL, a former Hitler Youth who was a soldier in the war and knew how to handle all arms, heavy guns and bazookas (Panzerfaust). He appointed two Colonels and they appointed four Lieutenants, the rest of us were just plain "soldiers."

The purpose of each gang was to make "war" on another gang. So, every so often, another street gang would invade our turf and this was "just cause" to start a war. In that case, a messenger was sent to the General of the offending gang and a challenge was issued. Then, at an appointed time and an appointed place the two gangs would meet. We would line up in single file, to show our numeric superiority, and we would shout insults at one another. Sometimes the confrontation ended there.

However, at other times the confrontation would be taken to an entirely new level, of actual war. That is, after the insults were shouted and nobody yielded, our leaders would select a small, bombed out street and we would occupy one side while the opponents would occupy the other. Then, we would throw "rocks" at each other. And, when "rock throwing" had little results we would elevate the conflict and use real guns with live ammunition. In one such encounter, one of our Colonels used a Panzerfaust to blow our opponents ruin into smithereens.

I was literally "shell shocked" and vowed from that day on not to continue with their antics. Luckily, in that incident no one was hurt seriously, but eventually many gang members of our street got seriously hurt. One lost his left arm, another his right hand and still another one eye.

So, instead I chose scouting and joined a Scouting group in our area. We made frequent trips to the outskirts of Berlin and I became very fond of Scouting.

Meanwhile, neither street gangs nor Scouting could satisfy the daily "drang" and be the outlet of the daily energy one has when one is young. So, a sport emerged and it took Berlin by storm. It was called Köppen.

The game used a Tennis ball and two players were needed. Two goals were marked, about 20 to 30 feet apart, and each player would have his turn in an alternating fashion the opportunity to score a goal. Thus, in an alternating fashion one was the attacker, the one with the ball, while the other was the defender of his goal. Only the attacker could score a goal.

The game would begin, when the attacker got the ball, threw it in the air and with his head gave it a "kick" trying to score a point. If the defender caught the ball cleanly, the "inning" was over and the defender became the attacker with the roles reversed.

However, when the defender only slapped the ball to the ground, the attacker could use a "soccer style" after kick to score. In short, it was a combination of "HEAD BALL" and soccer. Of course, if the head kick missed its mark, it was an "out" and the inning was over. The usual game lasted until 21 points were scored, sort of like in Ping Pong, with the exception that each turn did not necessarily result in a score.

Of course, the older boys dominated the game. I was 9, going on 10 when the game became popular. And, practically everybody older would beat me. So, I was determined to become the best player in our block. For, fame, glory and honor belonged to the champion.

After much cogitation, I determined to use my assets to buy a tennis ball. Then, to practice incessantly until I could beat everybody in our block, young and old alike. Now, to buy a tennis ball was not a small undertaking. The ball needed to be practically new so that it would bounce properly. And, even for me this was a major purchase because, Berlin was denuded of EVERYTHING, and in particular of tennis balls. And, to acquire a tennis ball would set me back at least 100 Marks, which to the average "bear" on our street was a fortune.

Of course, the first step was to get word out on "the street" that I was in the market for a tennis ball. And, as soon as I did, I had all kinds of offers with some of the most outrageous price demands. Some wanted up to 1000 Marks for a beat up ball. But, here my negotiating skills, which I had acquired in dealing with stamps, came in handy. I would casually, show the cash, and knock down the price to a ridiculous amount, to about 20 Marks if I liked the ball. Some sellers were actually offended by my counter offer, but I felt it was my money and I knew what the fair price was on the open market. So, after much bargaining and "horse trading" I got what I wanted at the price I was willing to pay. As you can see here on a small scale the Black Market in Berlin was alive and well.

Once I had my tennis ball, my status in the street changed immediately. I had what everybody wanted and needed for it was a "prima" tennis ball with a terrific bounce and with all the fuzz still on the ball. For all practical purposes it was a new ball. And, nobody on our street owned a new tennis ball. Very selectively, I would lend out my tennis ball and my status rose even higher. Meanwhile, I practiced feverishly to excel in the game.

First, I practiced my head shot. For it was critical, so I thought, to have the most powerful, practically unstoppable head shot. The reason was obvious, if I could score with my head shot, then I did not need the after shot because here the older boys had a distinct advantage over me. Some were accomplished soccer players and I felt I would not be able to out dribble them in the game. I needed both power and accuracy in my head shot.

We had a very wide staircase which led to our apartment in "The Fortress." So, I marked the corners of the first five steps and practiced my head shot on the staircase. Eventually, I got so good that I could head kick the ball into any desired corner of my choice. And, as I practiced, my shots got stronger and stronger.

Next, I practiced catching the ball cleanly, so that my opponent would be denied the after shot. Pretty soon, I started to excel in that also. Then, when I felt good and ready I challenged the champion of our street for a match.

He only laughed at me and said in effect, "I don't accept challenges from a pip squeak." Instead, I had to play the "pecking order" of the street. I agreed, and crushed the first few opponents. Within six months I had eliminated all players but our street champion. My meteoric rise, in the Köppen hierarchy of our street drew crowds when I played and I became the "darling" as I crushed much older players over 14 to 18 years of age.

My theory proved right. My head kick was practically unstoppable and my defense bordered on goalie acrobatics. Finally, a date was set to play our champion, and I must say our entire street and some players of our neighboring streets came to watch the "title match." I won and became the undisputed champion of our street.

So, here I was, the "pip squeak" 10 years old, who ruled KLOPSTOCK street in the game of Köppen. Even when I entered the GYMNASIUM in Berlin, I wielded authority since I became the player to beat. And, only on one occasion I lost to a "PRIMANER" in a heated match in the school. But, my days in Berlin were numbered, just as I had achieved status and "fortune."

In 1949, we left Berlin for West Germany and I had to build up my reputation from the bottom of the "Totem Pole." Primarily, losing my stamp business upset me for a long time. And, in addition, to my "schreck," no body in West Germany played my favorite game of Köppen.

Thus, I had to make my mark starting again from square one.

Stamps, My Favorite Hobby

My favorite hobby is collecting STAMPS. Yes, the kind you lick and stick, and when you need one most you don't have one to put on that urgent letter you are about to mail. Or, I am living in the past, where stamps have lost their usefulness as the INTERNET has taken over? Well, I don't think so, and while I am in the forefront of the present day technocrats I think the internet will never replace the intimacy of the written word and therefore, letter writing is here to stay. So, if you accept this premise, stamp collecting is here to stay also. In fact, it has been growing exponentially this century.

Let's do some basic "bean counting" to scope out the field. First, the number of collectors has been estimated to be 300 million or so world wide, and 6.5 million in America. This translates to about 2.3% of the population in America and less than .5% world wide.

However, stamp collecting requires some money, some literacy and plenty of leisure time, and this is where the basic statistics fail us. Because, in certain parts of our globe illiteracy is rampant, poverty is widespread and leisure time virtually non existent. I partition our globe into 5 collecting areas:

1) The Anglo Saxon world and their colonies, this includes USA, Great Britain and their former or present colonies.

2) Western Europe, this includes: France, Germany, Italy, Portugal, Spain etc. and their former or present colonies.

3) Eastern Europe, this includes: ROSSIJA (Russia), Czechoslovakia, Hungary, Poland, Ukraine etc and their former and present possessions, as they had no colonies, but only occupations by force.

4) Latin America, this includes the A,B,C countries Argentina, Brazil, Colombia and so on. They had no colonies, in fact until very recently most were colonies themselves.

5) This leaves us with a handful of independent countries of Africa and Asia, such as: Afghanistan, China, Egypt, Ethiopia, Liberia, Japan, Persia, Thailand, Turkey etc.

In all, while there are only 212 countries represented in the UNITED NATIONS. There were or still are, over 600 stamp issuing entities!!! In fact, it is the greatest privilege to issue stamps, which is governed by the UPU (Universal Postal Union), which was reconfirmed after the war in 1949. It is in effect a license to issue MONEY. Some countries misuse this privilege and print all the stamps the market will bear, to raise HARD CURRENCY. Most notably, the Eastern European countries and the former colonial nations which have gained their independence. The problem with this tactic is they actually ruin their marginal currency even more!

So, the 300 million collectors, when discounted for all its faults leaves us with about 150 million collectors in the HARD CURRENCY countries: USA, Canada, Great Britain, Western Europe, Japan and the PACIFIC RIM countries: Australia, Hong Kong, Korea, New Zealand, Singapore and Taiwan.

In Western Europe, stamp collecting is not merely a hobby but a serious investment medium. There, many a millionaire made his fortune in stamps. There, it is viewed as an international medium of exchange. For example, when Italy went recently through its disastrous inflation spiral, from 600 Lira to the Dollar, to 2500 Lira to the Dollar within a few years, smart money converted their LIRA to stamps, brought them out to Switzerland and sold them in the major auction houses. While the borders were closed for all jewels, art objects, gold and silver, stamps crossed the border undetected and unchallenged.

Many years ago a movie was made along these lines, it was called CHARADE. At that time 250,000 Dollars worth of stamps were pasted on a small envelope and nobody could find the loot. I like the movie very much.

Some estimates say that roughly 5 Billion Dollars was "salvaged" that way by savvy Italian collectors!!! As you can see, with this kind of numbers stamp collection ceases to be a hobby for kids but becomes a serious business. Accordingly, the number of serious collectors is very high in Western Europe, often claiming that 20 to 25% of the population collects stamps! I know for a fact that this is true in GERMANY. During the last century the entire savings of an average GERMAN were totally wiped out, while stamp prices rose meteorically!!!

Before I share some personal experiences with you let me point out that if you collect stamps you are in the "BEST of COMPANIES." Queen Elizabeth is an ardent stamp collector, so was FDR, so was King Farouk and so was the Shah of Persia and many more, the list could be endless.

In fact, my claim is that any HISTORIAN of name must also be a stamp collector of repute. Why? Stamp collecting has been around for over 160 years and, each country has flaunted its achievements, goals and aspirations in stamps. That is, they left behind MONUMENTS of their regime, which unlike the Egyptian obelisks, can not be erased or altered but remain there for humanity to see, FOREVER!

Thus, while many stamp purists may pontificate on the "purity" of the hobby, the plain fact remains: Each time a "STAMP STORY" hits the news, millions of neophytes start their journey into the world of stamp investing. If stamps had been invented by NOAH we would have today the most accurate HISTORY putting our existing history books to shame, and probably the most rarest stamps.

That is, from the earliest days, letters were forwarded and sometimes even delivered. But, the problem was that the receiver had to pay the cost of delivery. So, more frequently than not, the receiver did not have the money and could not accept the letter. By 1840, in London alone, a myriad of warehouses held a nearly uncountable number of letters which could not be delivered.

It took the genius of Postmaster Sir Rowland Hill to break with tradition and install an entirely new system and method of delivery. Rather than the recipient paying an absorbent price for a letter, the sender had to "prepay" a minuscule amount, one penny for London and her immediate suburbs, to send a letter. The recipient paid nothing, hence from that day on and to this day the recipient got his mail for free. So, from now on, ALL MAIL was in fact delivered, except for a few pathological cases.

Suppose you would like to study the "Inflation Spiral" we are on right now. Then, all you have to do is get a copy of a Stamp Catalogue for the United States and track the progress of the face values of the US Postage stamps. All we will track is the stamp for a first class mail and we have:

> 2 cent era ended in 1922
> 3 cent era from 1922 to 1957, or 35 years.
> 4 cent era from 1957 to 1963, or 6 years.
> 5 cent era from 1963 to 1968, or 5 years.
> 6 cent era from 1968 to 1971, or 3 years.
> 8 cent era from 1971 to 1973, or 2 years.
> 10 cent era from 1973 to 1976, or 3 years.
> 13 cent era from 1976 to 1978, or 2 years.
> ...etc. Today we are approaching the 50 cent era.

You can readily see that the increases get larger and the time interval shorter. That is within the next 50 years, or by 2064, we will probably need $5.00 to mail a letter. Thus, a strong case can be made that the postal system as it is today will become obsolete.

During the war (WWII) we lived in BERLIN (1943 to 1949), and when the war ended BERLIN was totally devastated. We lived in a "bombed out" building it was formerly the

REICHSGESUNDHEITSAMT. My stepfather GEORGE, called it "THE FORTRESS. Practically all buildings around us were totally bombed out. But, as soon as the war ended, reconstruction began. And, out of nowhere sprang up recycle stores. Practically everything was recyclable, copper, wrought iron, steel, keys and many other sundry items. At that time I was 7 going on 8 and in dire need of a few "shekels."

So, I build myself a mini wagon, staked out a ruin and started to dig for anything salable in the recycle shop. Then, I would load my wagon, and by the end of the day I would haul my "goodies" to the nearby store and convert it into CASH. So, one day as I was on one of my "digs" I found something stunning. It turned out to be a stamp collection. A few albums with stamps mounted in them, about a dozen or so stock books loaded with stamps and a few shoe boxes loaded with hundreds of envelopes, each with hundreds of stamps in them. I knew right away that I had stumbled onto something extraordinary. So, I interrupted my dig, loaded my find on my wagon and hauled it home. There, I had a bombed out room which I used for storage. I made a secret "vault" and hid my find there. Then, I returned to my dig and made sure I had salvaged all the goodies.

By the end of the day I took my regular haul to the recycle store, pocketed my cash and returned home. For a few days I was pounding my brain how to tell my mother. I was afraid she would confiscate my find, or give it away or some such thing, as she had often done before. This time I was determined to keep most of it and yet "operate in the open." Already, my older sister called me "CROESUS" because I was ALWAYS IN THE MONEY. And, I was already the virtual "banker" in our family. Everybody envied me for my money yet, at the same time they would "ridicule" my business in some way.

However, neither George nor my sister would go out and dig, while my mother worked as a nurse from dawn to dusk. When my mother was in a bind, I would share my profits from the digs with her, but only with her. And, she never took all the money but always left me enough for my own use.

My sister was different, when I returned, she would greet me with, "And, how has Croesus made out today?..." Then, she would tell me her sob story of the day and I would part with a few Marks. My income was "fantastic" for the time and place. I could often bring home more that 100 Marks, which was more than my mother earned. But, by absolute standards it was a pittance. For, 100 Marks one could buy at most four packs of AMERICAN CIGARETTES or about $1.00. And, after I paid everybody off, I was left with maybe 10 or 20 Marks.

Still, when you consider that I made that every day, I had a bankroll of "enormous" proportions. Very soon I had more than 1000 Marks and I felt like CROESUS.

Finally, I came up with a way to bring my stamp find into the open, for I was determined to make a business of it. So one day, I took one album and one shoe box and "revealed" its contents to my mother. She did not know what to do. My revelation, however, caused a mild commotion in our flat. First, she tried to find out who the owner was. No doubt she wanted me to return it to him. However, in the end, reason prevailed and it was decided that "WE" could keep it, sort of like, war booty.

But, to my amazement, it was also determined that the collection was too valuable for me to keep. So, the compromise became that I could keep the shoe box, which had many more stamps but, the collection I had to sell to my sister for 2 Marks!!! I don't know to this day how they came up with this formula. But, in the end, I was satisfied because now I could "operate" openly. My mother had found a Solomonian solution and my sister became a proud owner of a collection to which she had no claim whatsoever, except by the right of being "firstborn." She was 7 year older.

When school started in the fall, the digs became useless. It became increasingly more difficult to find "virgin" ruins to dig in. In fact the city government now organized "chain gangs," mostly prisoners of war who began to clean up the ruins systematically. Also, school left me with much less time. In practical terms, digs became more difficult, less rewarding and much more dangerous, often with exposed live ammunition.

So, now I started on my second phase. What to do with my collection? In school I asked a few classmates if they collected stamps. And, to my amazement they all did. In fact one introduced me to a stamps dealer. The stamp dealer loaned me a catalog and now I could determine exactly what my stamps were worth. With great difficulty I cataloged one envelope and to my utter disbelief that envelope catalogued over 100 Marks. I took my "handy work" to the dealer and he explained to me that the catalog serves as a reference rather than the actual value. And, that the actual value was somewhere between half and one third of the catalog value.

However, at the same time the dealer offered to "buy" some of my stamps and sell me others at a great discount. Naturally, I took a few envelopes and one stock book to him. He picked out what he wanted and gave me a huge hoard of stamps in return. Furthermore, he gave me great pointers on how to sell the stamps. I would fill a few stock book and sell them at a fixed price for 10 Pfennig each. I tried his method in school, and soon I had a brisk business during the lunch break and after school.

Then, one day a soldier, an American soldier, saw me trading stamps and offered to buy some from me. But, he offered to pay in American currency, one penny a piece. I agreed and he bought practically my entire stock book, about 5 dollars worth! In German currency that was a fortune, the equivalent of 20 packs of American cigarettes. Most importantly, he made an appointment for next week and so my stamp business flourished until we left Berlin in 1949.

When we left Berlin, I had two suitcases. One contained my personal stuff; the other contained my stamps. Our first stop was in Cornberg. It was a DP camp which was about to be dissolved. All the people there had already been accepted to the USA, Canada or Australia. For us it was a temporary stop, since George and Emilia had to be "de nazified," and American intelligence was in Southern Bavaria, in Mittenwald and in Oberammergau. Besides, Emilia was not with us; she was with Emma who was in a cast in a Hospital. And they were flown to Wiesbaden.

When I started exploring the stamp situation, nobody collected stamps. In fact they gave me all their mail and I saved all the stamps. I considered myself to be a true stamp collector. I collected only used stamps, in my collection (my stamp dealer friend taught me that). Naturally, I kept the mint stamps I had, but as far as I was concerned they were only "virtual" stamps. Let me explain.

There are two schools of thought about stamp collecting. One says, a stamp is only collectible when it has been used or was cancelled. Then, what is important is the cancellation. And, if the city and date is not readable in the cancel then the cancellation is called a "favor" cancellation. For valuable stamps that cancellation can make all the difference in price. In general, "favor" cancellations sell at a fraction of a properly cancelled stamp.

The other school of thought is when a collector collects mint stamps. In collecting circles these collectors are also called investors. This is so, because the true function of the stamp has not yet been exercised. In particular, in Europe all stamps have a "period of validity." That is, if one does not use a stamp during its period of validity its franking value expires. Thus, technically the stamp is worthless. Mint collectors collect stamps for their "artistic value." But, what is most important in a mint stamps is its "GUM." Thus, when the gum is disturbed in any way, the price of the stamp is only a fraction of the mint value.

In addition to this, the overall condition of the stamp is very important. Again, a defective stamp fetches only a fraction of a perfect stamp. A defect can be a tear, a fold, a crease, a discoloration, fading from the sun's rays and so on.

As you can see, once you become a stamp collector you have to learn quickly all the qualitative aspects and the discounts associated with each. I hope you can readily see there is ample room for "horse trading."

After a few months we were moved to Fulda. There Emilia found us, and we made arrangements to move to Mittenwald. Our stay in Fulda was too brief and I was not able to establish any stamp contacts.

Finally, we arrived in Mittenwald. Again, we had to stay in a DP Camp and I was sent to the only school there, which was a Ukrainian school. We arrived there in late 1949, as I recall, in mid September. Actually, there were two camps, both were former German military compounds: "Jägerkaserne and Pionierkaserne."

Emilia worked in a nearby hospital where Emma stayed. George refused to work, because we were there on the orders of the US Government. Thus, all payments were deducted from Emilia's salary. In effect Emilia worked for nothing. Undaunted, she took a second job, a private duty job. Then, she was approached by one of Bandera's men. They needed a nurse and since she was Ukrainian she was elected. Emilia accepted and was paid in cash and in goods. The only problem was, their hospital was given to them in secret by the Americans and nobody was allowed to go there. So, a driver would arrive daily, meet Emilia, put on a blindfold on Emilia and drive her to the secret hospital. When her shift was up, the driver would come back, meet Emilia, blindfold her and drive her home.

Again, both camps were being dissolved. In June 1950, my Ukrainian School closed and I had to transfer to a German Real Gymnasium in Oberammergau. All who stayed behind had to go to Oberammergau and take an exam for the class grade they wanted to attend. About 50 students from the Ukrainian School showed up for the exam. As it turned out I passed for the 3rd grade and three sisters passed for the 3rd, 4th and 5th grade. We were the only ones who passed. So, starting in September the four of us would walk from the Pionierkaserne to the train station in Mittenwald. Pretty soon I walked with Olga (the 3rd grader) hand in hand to the train station.

But this came to an abrupt end when Emilia and George were cleared and released in January 1951. Emilia had a patient who left her a key to a four room flat in Munich. It was a former castle of the Wittelsbach. But, since it was bombed out, squatters had occupied the castle. And, Emilia had secured one of the squatters apartments. The location was terrific.

The castle was right at the edge of the "English Garden," a great park in the midst on Munich, and one block to the tramway.

Emilia had a job waiting for her and I was sent to the Real Gymnasium in Munich.

Once I settled in I inquired about some stamp action. Low and behold practically everybody collected stamps. And, the school had a stamp club to boot. I had arrived in "Stamp Heaven."

31

As it turned out, the school was getting ready for a "Stamp Exhibition." There was very little time for me to put together a really nice collection for the exhibit but I did the best I could. I had by far the most expensive stamps exhibited. But there was one student who designed his own pages, described every stamp in beautiful black ink. He got the first prize. But, I got the second prize.

The exhibition was sponsored by a large adult stamp club. They gave out the prizes and the first three winners in our school exhibit were also invited to join the adult stamp club for free, like honorary members. I thought that was great and I went to their next meeting. There, I met Hans.

Hans was a soldier in Russia during the war. He was wounded and captured in Germany. After his release, which was only a few months ago, he got a job at the Mayor's office. He was in charge of all the mailings, in particular the return mail. Thus, every month he took home a sack full stamp clippings. He sorted them, washed them, dried them and stored them in envelopes in shoe boxes. When I met him he had practically one room full of shoe boxes stacked away.

I was more than exited when he told me all this. Then I volunteered to walk home with him. I had a bike, so I pushed the bike while he walked leisurely along. To me it was obvious what he needed but I did not want to be too pushy. So, I asked him anyway, "Have you considered selling some of these stamps?"

Hans replied, "I don't have the time, but I am looking for somebody who will work with me." This was music to my ears. I continued right away, "Why don't you make up a stock book with material you want to sell, you set the price and I will sell it for you."

"That's wonderful," I heard and then he continued "when can you come to my place?" Well, the rest was duck soup. The next day, after school I was at his apartment. He had prepared 3 stock books full of stamps. Then, he offered a "pricing formula:" definitives and commemorative (all stamps without an additional charge) at 50% face value; semipostals for full face value. And, my commission was to be 20% of the sale. I thought this was the most generous offer I ever had.

I looked at the stock books and I knew I would have no problem whatsoever. Every stamp was almost perfectly cancelled. To a collector this was paradise. The total value of the three stock books was a few thousand D Marks using his formula. But, I knew that on many of the semipostals I could get much more. I told him so. He just shrugged his shoulder and said, "You get more, you keep the difference."

The next day, after school I rode on my bicycle to the first dealer right in the middle of town. I waited patiently for my turn, then I asked him if he was interested in modern Germany. Well, to make a long story short, he bought all three books with a huge premium for the semipostals.

I decided to wait a few days. I was afraid to return so soon having sold everything so quickly. On the third day I went to see him. I showed him the full amount I got. Then, he paid my commission, and we split the overage! And, he had another 3 books ready for me! Needless to say this was truly a bonanza for me and for him. Pretty soon we operated on a regular schedule: Monday and Wednesday were my "pick up" days and pay days.

On my next sales trip I went to a different dealer. Again I sold everything. Then, I made it a point to develop about ten buyers. This way I would not overpower each individual dealer.

The money was "rolling in" and I started to build out my own collection. That became my "nest egg."

Unfortunately nothing lasts forever. In February 1957, the KGB nearly caught George, in broad daylight, in the middle of the town (near the "Marienkirche"). A taxi pulled up, two men jumped out and tried to drag George into their taxi. George resisted the best he could and screamed from the top of his lungs. Bystanders rushed to his help and "tore him away from the clutches of the KGB" (that was how George described it). He came in a taxi, shaking like a leaf. Emilia calmed him down and together they went to the American Embassy, applied for asylum and applied to emigrate to America. Their request was accepted and we were allowed to leave within 30 days!

This caught everybody in the family by surprise. I did not want to go at that time. I was five months away from graduating from the

Oberrealschule, which made me "one of the most eligible bachelors" in Munich. My stamp business was booming, I would have to give it up. I was not going to go and that was it.

Emma was in a similar position. She was working for Radio Liberty and a prolonged absence could cost her dearly. But, we were outvoted, because Emilia, George, and Kathy wanted to go; only Emma and I refused. But, after much negotiating both Emma and I caved in for the "sake of the greater good for the family." Actually, George was "transferred," to the New York Office.

Then, I told myself, "surely there are stamp collectors in America, maybe I could have even a more lucrative business there! I told Hans, my stamp supplier, how kismet had changed my status and I could do nothing about it. Emilia had put her foot down and changed my life irrevocably. But I told Hans that I would find buyers in New York and we would conduct our business by mail, to which he agreed.

When we arrived in New York City and I went on a "Stamp Dealer hunt," I had the biggest disappointment of my life. To begin with, most collectors in America collected mint stamps. (To me that was "gum collecting"). And, most important of all, nobody cared for the "cancellations." Any cancellation seemed to be acceptable. The whole beauty and intricacy of stamp collecting was lost. (Only now, in the 21st Century is America beginning to recognize the value and meaning of a proper cancellation). Of course to a large degree the Post Office is at fault. They suggest a spot on the envelope to stick your stamp on, but then they use a "killer cancellation" to deface the stamp while the city and date are at the "far end!" You don't know how many letters I have written to the Postmaster General pointing out that each year they are killing at least 5 billion dollars worth of stamps this way. But, as you can see, THEY DON'T CARE."

To begin with, German stamps were much cheaper in America than in Germany. Pretty soon I figured out that stamps in their own country fetch the highest prices. Thus, here was a ready made business to travel to various countries and make money. In general, the differential is at least 20%. And, for better items and pairs, strips of three or blocks of four the difference could be as high as 100%!!! Especially when it comes to "classics". But that business was not for me, because it also required a substantial capital investment of $10,000 or more to be effective.

America, unlike Europe has many catalogues; primarily Scott and Minkus. But these catalogue makers make their money not from the catalogue business but from printing album pages to hold stamps. That is, pre printed pages. By definition you can have different catalogue makers if they use a different numbering system. Since the first catalogue, Gibbons by name, was created in England they have a patent on their numbering system. The next catalogue was Michel, a German catalogue. It had a different numbering system. Then came Scott. Since they were last they had to invent a different numbering system. It is called in the trade as the "alphabet soup" numbering system. Let me explain.

Stamps are issued for many different occasions. For example: Definitives are stamps that have the entire range of the possible denominations required. In the USA that could be from 1/4 cent stamp (used for newspapers) all the way up to a $5.00 stamp (used for certification, insurance and so on).

The next category is called "Commemorative" stamps. They are issued to commemorate special events. Then, there are Semipostals. These are stamps with two values, one is the franking value the other is a donation to a Government charity. Then, there are Airmail stamps. They had to be used if you wanted your mail to be delivered by air. And, so on. The number of such "subdivision" is nearly endless. Thus, Scott lumped the definitives and commemorative into one category and provided an alphabetic prefix for all other categories. Thus, the prefix B was used for semipostals and the prefix C was used for airmails and so on.

Stamp collectors have always distinguished between stamps and dues. Dues, while they look like stamps, are a form of "penalty." That is, the sender used the wrong amount on the letter, and the postage due stamp showed the amount due. Many collectors do not collect the dues so they are in the "back of the book" for each country.

The most universal catalogue in Europe is Michel, because it is very comprehensive and the most universal in the USA is Scott, because it is the cheapest. Minkus came late to the game. He organized his catalogue from a different perspective, from that of a stamp investor. The usual process a stamp investor used was to "pick a country" of his choice for investment, because the period from 1945 to 1956 had meteoric rise in stamp values, and subscribe at the main post office for all stamps issued by that country. For example: Berlin, Germany, Saar; Italy, San Marino, Vatican; France, Andorra (French); Spain, Andorra (Spanish) and Portugal and so on.

Then, he would receive every stamp whenever it was issued in the desired quantity. Practically every country has this kind of subscription service. But, then the stamps the subscriber would receive was not governed by any specific type, but every type in the chronological order is was issued. They only feature Minkus added was to group them by sets!

At first the organization seems ridiculous to a stamp collector simply because it lumps stamps and dues (and all other categories) together. In addition, Minkus overpriced the "hot issues of the hot countries." In time Minkus made a run for the dominance of the stamp market in the USA. Unfortunately, Minkus had a special deal with Gimbels; he ran a very successful stamp store at Gimbels. But, when Gimbels was sold, Minkus lost his store and the appeal for his catalogue. However, his pre printed pages continued to grow in volume. That is, more and more collectors like his geopolitical groupings of "stamp issuing entities;" which nobody else does. For example, suppose you collect Portugal and its colonies. Then, if you don't use Minkus, you would be hard pressed to put all the colonies together. The same applies for Germany, Italy, Spain, Russia and many more countries.

However, stamp collections are eventually sold. Since the focus in the USA is Scott, the Minkus organization is foreign to most dealers and buyers. They often miss the key stamps in a Minkus collection. Thus, the trick is easy. If you want to make money, you buy only Minkus collections. Your collection must be in Scott Specialty pages (these are the premium pages). Then you transfer the stamps you are missing to your collection. The remainder you can easily resell in the collector's market. All you have to do is to subscribe to a collector's newspaper, such as Linns and you are in business.

How do you put a price on the collections you try to resell? Easy, get a sales list from dealers who sell "packages," such as Subway. That is, a certain number of stamps at a fixed price. Price your lot at least 20% below the going price. For example, suppose 1,000 Portugal and colonies sell for $100 and you have a lot of 1021 stamps for Portugal and colonies. Then, charge $80 and you will readily sell them. When there are better stamps in the lot (over $10 catalogue) then list them that they are part of your lot and charge a little more. Of course the harder way is to catalogue each stamp, tally the total and try to sell them at 1/4 catalogue (Scott).

However, the key to a successful stamp business is to hook up with a larger, more experienced dealer or even an auction house. Then, you will flourish in no time.

I have described only one aspect of selling stamps in the USA. Nowadays there are many, many more aspects. For example, collect errors, freaks and forgeries. In other words the opportunities are endless.

When you get started, find yourself an auction house you can work with. In a world wide Minkus collection you should find at least 200 countries and it may cost you $3,000 dollars net. But, it should be bulging with stamps.

First, pick the countries you want to collect. Say you begin with USA, Canada, Great Britain and the British commonwealth. Then, these are the counties you take out for your own collection. These countries you put into a Scott Specialty binder using Scott Specialty pages, they command a premium when you sell your collection. And, eventually EVERYBODY sells their collection!

The pages don't have to be preprinted, blank pages will be fine. Don't overcrowd the pages, no more than 30 stamps per page in chronological order is tops. For that you will need a catalogue. If you buy a used catalogue, 2 to 5 years old, you will save yourself a lot of money, it's much better to put the money into stamps than into stamp supplies.

Ok, this gets you started. Now group the countries with the most stamps in them for sale. Make up at least 60 lots. Describe and price each lot. So your sales list should be about 6 to 10 pages long. Make 25 or 30 copies. Then advertize in a stamp newspaper, a small 3 or 4 line add will do.

When you get an inquiry, send out your sales list and wait for a reply. If you priced your lots well you will sell about half. That is, 30 lots at an average price of $100 makes $3000 dollars return.

With the first few sales you have to build up your capital so that you can spend about $5,000 with your auction dealer. At that price level you will get good service and good recommendations. Often some "unsold lots" will go very cheap, in particular if they are on Minkus pages.

In general, you should be able to make three times the money you spend. Of which one third goes into your collection, one third into your inventory and one third into your sales list. In time you may add more countries to your collection.

Many dealers started this way. Figure this way, every 10 years your collection should grow to $100,000.00, your medium income should be $15,000.00 and your inventory should grow to $50,000.00. Thereafter, your collection should double in value every 10 years. Thus if you collect for 30 or 40 years, you will build up a sizable nest egg.

Downstream you may find it inconvenient to work your duplicates from pre printed pages. Then, dealers and collectors resort to glassine envelopes. My preference are #2 envelopes. They are sufficiently small but hold at least 50 stamps. When you have more of one kind, use larger envelopes such as #4. They fit almost perfectly into a shoe box.

All these are useful hints for a beginner. Once you get started you will innovate on your own.

Good Luck!

Ivan Kornilovich Korniew, my Father

My recollection of my father is very sparse, I was 3 going on 4 when he was murdered by the Soviets. I remember only 3 events distinctly. The first was, when I was taken to an outing to the river DNIPRO (Dnieper when russified). From my perspective it was a HUGE body of water, I could not see the other shore even though everybody assured me that it was clearly visible by all adults. This may prove that grownups have a better long range vision than little folks.

The next event was during the war with Germany. By early August of 1941, the German STUKAS were strafing the outlying areas of Kiyiv (Kiev when russified.) The two properties of land Emilia had acquired were separated by a YAR or a massive ravine. Only on one corner was a tiny passage way which connected the two properties. In that ravine Ivan had built a BUNKER on the main property side of the ravine. Then, one day my father took me by the hand, led me to the bunker and explained that in case of an air attack I had to dash into the bunker and hide inside. And, if I could not make it to the bunker, but only to the ravine, then to use the ravine itself as a shelter. And always lay flat on the side the airplanes were coming from. Then, we PRACTICED for a while so I would know exactly what to do when my parents were not home.

The last time was, when my father was murdered near the passage way of the two properties in our wheat field which came up right to the passage way of the two properties. Then, Emilia took me there and showed me the trampled area of the wheat field were my father bled to death.

So, most of the information I have about my father and his family is second hand and comes from Emilia, my mother. His ancestors were very colorful. Ivan's grandfather was a secretary at the Zaporozhian SITCH. And, when the SITCH was finally disbanded in 1897 for the last time, he dug up his treasure, got himself a wife and bought a small farm in the OREL area. In addition to him, they included a WITCH, a BLUEBEARD, a HERMIT and a passionate INVENTOR with the most incredible gadgets.

It all started when the KORNIEWS, who were well to do farmers in the OREL area went to the PERESHEPIN FAIR with their only son ALEXIS. His father had pawned off his two daughters to the local monastery when they turned 19 and were still unmarried. He paid 200 rubles and a cow for each, so they would lead a life of relative leisure for the rest of their life at the monastery. It was taken for granted that any self respecting woman had to be married by the age of 18, unless she wanted to become an old maid, a witch or a nun. Thus, it was common practice for the well to do, to pawn off their unmarried daughters to a well respected monastery.

The "dowry" they brought determined their status in the monastery. Without a dowry, they became field workers. With 100 rubles, they became attendants. And, with 200 rubles and a cow they could lead a life of leisure.

Alexis was 17, good looking, blond and blue eyed, and the "most eligible bachelor" in the OREL area. At the FAIR he met DUNJA age 26, and fell madly in love with her. His parents were shocked, their only son married a WITCH! When we left KIYIV, Dunja was alive and well at 104! In fact, the year before, she walked in the 'dead of winter,' about 50 miles without batting an eyelash. They had four children one of whom became a hermit and died at age 92. Another, my grand father Kornilow, was a "BLUEBEARD." He would marry, and within a year his wife would die. This would repeat 7 times, and each time the wife would die within one year. It got to the point that nobody would give him their daughter in marriage anymore.

So, he went to the CRIMEA and BOUGHT himself a wife, NATALIE. She bore him three sets of twins, all one year apart. Then, she declared that from now on, he had to live in separate quarters and

NO MORE CHILDREN. So, Kornilov built himself a little cabin and dedicated himself to reading and inventing.

Each morning Natalie would bring him a full SAMOVAR of tea and a basket of food, and he was left alone. She took care of the farm, the children and all the farm animals. Eventually, two children died, and four survived. One married MARSHALL ZHUKOV, Nicholas attended the FRUNZE Academy (like WEST POINT), one became a Doctor of medicine, my aunt Poly. And, the last one was Ivan who was born in 1902 on Saint Ivan's day.

When WWI started, Ivan was too young to join. And, when the war ended in the Ukraine in 1917, Ivan was 15. By then he had finished high school with distinction. But instead of going to the University, he was eager to defend the Ukraine.

When the war ended, Ukraine's trouble began. Bands of deserters and regular troops roamed the countryside. A Czech army was moving east to liberate the Czar. A Rumanian army moved east also, trying to reach America via Shanghai. A Hungarian army roamed the countryside and a Bulgarian army tried to make it home.

To top them all, came the German occupation forces which the Russians approved when they signed the Treaty of Brest Litovsk in 1917 with the Germans. The Ukraine was given to the Germans as reparations for the war. The Ukraine was repeatedly used by Russia like a "monopoly piece of property" to satisfy an enemy. (The same tactic was used in the Treaty of Andrussovo with Poland in 1667 when Russia and Poland divided the Ukraine. The Poles came in, and forced even more conversions than before).

The Germans stayed until 1919. But, then erupted the civil war between WHITES (supporters of the Czar) and REDS, the supporters of the revolution. I think the Russian slogans eventually determined the outcome of the civil war. The slogan of the WHITES was: "Beat the Jews and save mother Russia," while the slogan of the REDS was: "All the land to the people."

The Ukrainian defense team came up with a strategy. They divided the Ukraine, west of the Dnipro River, into 50 kilometer squares (2500 square kilometers). And, each square was patrolled by a squad of 6 to 10 men and/or women on horseback. They would take on deserters but were forbidden to engage regular troops then they had to notify the defense team, and they would take the proper action. Ivan was attached to such a unit as he was an expert rider. In a short time, he became leader of his group.

He often spoke of his exploits. In particular of his "Maxim machine gun," which he called his "Bayan," a musical instrument.

Meanwhile, the UKRAINE tried to become independent, but none of her neighbors would let her. Poland, which was liberated by the Germans in 1917 invaded the western Ukraine in 1921, as did Hungary and Rumania, all of whom took territories from the Ukraine.

Then, when the Russians were not welcome in Kiyiv and the Ukraine, the REDS moved to KHARKIEV and declared it the Capital of the Ukraine. By 1921, the French, the British and a Czech armies roamed in the Ukraine, devastated the land, took the crops and livestock, and a terrible famine ensued.

By 1924, the REDS crushed whatever was left of an independent Ukraine, russified the Ukrainian DON and KUBAN and, in 1926 integrated them into "Mother Russia." (The same way they annexed the Crimea in 2014!)

His term was up after 4 years. When the REDS took over the Ukraine in 1925, the commandos were gradually phased out and most became heroes of "Communism." This service earned Ivan the right to attend a University and get an advanced degree, which he did. He was admitted to Kiyiv University on a "fast paced program." He took up CHEMISTRY, and eventually became one of the leading Chemists in the Ukraine and the Soviet Union.

In that capacity he was assigned as Chemist to a plant in ZINOVSK and eventually became the TECHNICAL DIRECTOR, with 107 patents to his name.

By 1927, at the age of 25, he became an important Chemist because he was turning out one patent after another. By 1930, he was a household name in the Soviet Union, and that is when he met Emilia.

While he was the leader of a commando, Ivan had a common law wife. And, when the commando was dismantled he developed ZINGA, from the "roaming lifestyle," a form of scurvy, with the prospect of losing his teeth and his hair. So, when he came home, his mother sent him to their doctor who could do nothing, the ZINGA was too advanced. But, he gave him some medication anyway.

Then, Natalia, his mother, told him to go to the local WITCH for a cure and remedy. And, he did.

The witch lived in the nearby woods, and was very famous for her cures. So, when he arrived she looked at him and said,
"You are not a God fearing man, but I see many good traits in you. So, I will help you despite yourself." Then, she brewed a concoction of "bark," put some of it in a bottle, gave him some "powder" and told him to eat as many cherries as he could lay his hands on, and to take her medication twice a day. He did what she said, and within a month the ZINGA was cured!

When Ivan transferred to ZINOVSK, his common law wife would not go with him, so they parted company but remained friends. She took a teaching job in Odessa.

As Ivan distinguished himself in his field, he got the attention of the Soviet military. They had concluded a treaty with Germany in Rapallo Italy. Rapallo is a small town in Italy. Starting in 1923, many treaties were negotiated and ratified there; in particular the treaty between Germany and the Soviet Union.

After Germany's defeat in World War I and the ensuing treaty of Versailles in 1919, Germany was not allowed to maintain a normal military, It was limited to 100,000 soldiers, and Germany was forbidden to develop weapons of war: tanks, rifles, airplanes, U boats and so on. Allied inspectors roamed throughout Germany, reported any and all violations and punished the perpetrators. Therefore, a viable alternative needed to be found, far away from the prying eyes of the Allied inspectors.

The German military began planning for a "REVANCHE" before the ink had died in the Versailles Treaty. They approached the Soviet Union. They found a receptive ear and met in Rapallo to discuss terms.

The Germans needed land far away from the Allied inspectors, and in exchange, they promised to share their technology. To keep everything "open" between them, they agreed to have their premises inspected by Soviet scientists and weapons specialists, both in the area given to them in the Soviet Union and in Germany, mainly with Porshe and his facilities, each year. Thus, the plans were developed in secret in Germany by men like Porshe and implemented in the Soviet Union. The German in charge in the Soviet Union was Heinz Guderian. The principal area given to Germans was near Kazan and a few other locations. Each area was fenced off and patrolled by Germans in Soviet uniforms. Whenever a German died accidentally, his remains were crated and shipped to Germany labeled "Defective Machine Parts."

Naturally, the entire operation was top secret, and only a select people knew about it. Thus from 1923 to 1933, the weapons development program was conducted by Germany in complete secrecy in the Soviet Union.

When Hitler came to power in 1933, he was invited by Guderian for a "show and tell" demonstration near Kazan. This was the first demonstration of "Blitzkrieg," a coordinated attack by infantry, tanks and air force. How was that possible? By short wave radio, of course. Every commander had a short wave radio and could detail each attack for each unit!!!

Hitler was flabbergasted and was jumping for joy. By 1935, all Rapalloland operations were moved to Germany and Hitler began his "REVANCHE."

How do I know this? My father was a member of the Soviet inspection team! How did he make it to that team? By 1930, my father

Ivan Kornilovich Korniew was the leading Soviet Chemist with over 100 patents to his name (the total was 107). And, he loved to go on the inspection tours because they were allotted western clothes: one overcoat, two suits, two pairs of shoes, two shirts, two belts, two ties, two pairs of socks and one hat of their choice...

Meanwhile, Emilia was taking a course in medicine in Odessa and occasionally she would travel by train to see her parents in Kharkiev. On one such trip she met Ivan. Ivan liked Emilia from the start and Emilia liked Ivan. So, they agreed to meet again on her return trip to Odessa. Emilia was late, but Ivan was still waiting for her. After a short courtship, they married.

(When I worked at BROOKHAVEN NATIONAL LAB., in UPTON NY, a delegation of chemists from the SOVIET UNION visited us. In that delegation, were many of his coworkers, but I refrained from making any contact with them).

In 1933, Ivan founded the Ukrainian Chemical Society. But in 1935 he inhaled noxious gases at the plant and got deathly sick. Now Emilia stepped in to his rescue and began the long recovery to good health. During his recuperation he lost his recognition, his apartment and other privileges. (Do you remember what happened to Boris Spassky when he lost to Bobby Fisher?) He was even deleted from the "International Who's Who" for 1935 and subsequent years. In the worker's paradise you work; and if you are maimed or wounded and unable to work, you are automatically excluded from that "paradise."

Emilia, my Mother

Emilia Korniew Kandiew
AN ODE TO ALL MOTHERS and in
particular to EMILIA, my Mother.

I am perpetually in awe of the bond mothers form with their new born children. This bond begins with the miracle of birth, when the scrawniest bundle of humanity is presented to the mother and no matter what its shape, form or size, an instant bonding occurs. And, when there are many children in the family, the one with the greatest need, usually gets the most attention. Emilia or my mother, was such a mother. She was exceptional in every respect. Despite all the adversities she encountered in her life, she never gave up and achieved all her goals. She came to AMERICA; her children got a higher education; all her children outlived her; she got an art degree in AMERICA, in addition to all her other degrees. She worked in the field she loved (medicine) and she retired in peace and relative comfort in Florida. Even in her old age, when she could no longer manage her affairs she was very happy when I decided to live with her, until she died, on August 27, 2001.

Her grandfather was ROZDAYBIDA (hand out some grief, a Cossack name), a scribe or secretary in the Zaporozhian Sich. His actual name was Taras Hordienko. He was married to Tamara, a gorgeous girl from the Kharkiev area. His daughter Anna, married a "russified" German, "Gabriel Grotte." The Grotte's came from the Wiesbaden area. They were three brothers. One was a "Master Sausage maker" in Germany and set up a factory near Kharkiev, from where he supplied Moscow with an unending supply of UKRAINIAN sausage. (Ukrainian sausage is similar to Polish Kielbasa, except it has much more garlic in it). He claimed that each shipment to Moscow, could be laid out in sausage, yard for yard, for about 200 miles.

The other brother, Gabriel, was a structural engineer, who set up an engineering firm near Saltov, but later moved to Kiyiv (Kiev when russified). The third brother was Max, who managed the sausage factory for his older brother for a while, he was a surveyor and metallurgical engineer by training, but he was also an efficient bookkeeper and accountant by necessity. The Grotte's changed their name to a good Russian name in order to be inconspicuous in the Ukraine.

In 1910, Gabriel married Anna, and with her dowry of 20,000 gold rubles and his savings they bought a prime estate of about 3,000 hectares (about 5 to 6,000 acres) near Kharkiev, called:
"KRYNYZHNAYA." The estate was famous for its wells, as people flocked to them from near and far for the purity of the water. And, all visitors were allowed to take as much water as they could carry away, free of charge. (And, until my mother's death, she would not skimp on the purity and taste of water but, always bought the best water money could buy, in Florida it was, CAROLINA SPRING WATER, at $1.35 per gallon).

Emilia was born with a "silver spoon" in her mouth. Her mother Anna was a successful art dealer; her father Gabriel was a very successful structural engineer who specialized in "bridge building." Gabriel had two brothers Max and Leonhard. They were Germans who came to Russia/ Ukraine to make their fortune, by invitation of the Czarist government. Their original name was Grotte, and they came from the Wiesbaden area. When they arrived in the Ukraine, they took (with government permission) a good sounding Russian name.

Anna met Gabriel at a country fair and fell madly in love.
When they married, her father gave Anna a dowry of 20,000 Rubles in gold. With that money, they bought a large estate outside of Kharkiev. The feature of the estate was a main house, a guest house, a huge apple orchard with "Antonov Apples," which paid the tax bill and was the primary source of income.

About 1/3 rd of the estate was developed, the other 2/3 rd was a forrest. Each year about 100 acres of forrest was sold for timber and then replanted with seedlings. In this way, the forrest was self regenerating. The rest of the estate flaunted an apple orchard, about 90 acres of ANTONOV apples. They were the most desirable variety in the Ukraine. And, in effect they sold "apple futures" every year, thus passing their maintenance to the buyer. That is, right after the apple trees bloomed and the first growth was visible, buyers came; they estimated the crop (also using the actual crop of the prior year), then they would bid on the future crop. Of course, the highest bidder bought the future crop and it was his responsibility to maintain the orchard and harvest the crop.

The apples were the mainstay of the estate. They paid for all the expenses with plenty of cash left over. In addition, there was an orchard of WALNUTS, about 50 acres which were sold in the same manner. About 1000 acres, were used to grow wheat, barely, corn and sunflowers. Here, the entire 1000 acres were "rented for 1/3 of the crop" to a farmer or farming combine. And, finally, about 200 acres were used for private use, these included, landscaped grounds around the main house, a garden for vegetables, strawberries and gooseberries, and an area for the farm animals, which included about 30 cows, 10 horses, 100 pigs, a flock of geese and lots of chickens.

The entire estate was managed by Anna. When Max gave up his job in his brother's sausage factory he resumed his main profession as surveyor, and helped out on the estate. Anna kept three families in the "little" house, and with 6 workers or so, she maintained the entire estate.

The main house stood recessed on a hill, surrounded by a landscaped garden, overlooking the entire estate. From a wrap around porch all the activities could be observed and all visitors spotted well before they arrived. The house featured 7 grecian columns and 18 rooms. One room housed an extensive library while another featured Anna's favorite hobby, she collected paintings.

One time, Anna bought a very famous painting by SARATOV, called "A letter to the Sultan," by the Zaporozhian Cossacks. This depicted an actual historical event, when the Sultan of the Ottoman

Empire, wrote to the Cossacks requesting a cessation of their raids into the Crimea and to the shores of the BLACK SEA. The Sultan wanted to negotiate a potential peace. But, from the Cossack's point of view, they were only liberating mostly Ukrainian captives, taken at wanton Tartar raids. And, since they did not believe the sincerity of the Sultan, their response was: "The moon shines on you and us, therefore kiss our ASS," which is loosely translated.

Into this milieu EMILIA was born on September 12, 1912, with much jubilation. But, within a few years, Russia was drawn into a war that changed everything. By the time she was 5, in 1917, WW I was nearing its end for Imperial Russia. Schools were closing as "all able bodied persons" were drafted as cannon fodder to the front. Armed with wooden toy rifles, with no ammunition, they were sent to the front. There, they were to capture the weapons of the Germans and fight them to the bitter end. So, do you find it surprising that the Czarist regime was hated in the Ukraine?

Nevertheless, both Gabriel and Anna, started to educate Emilia at home. When the war actually ended, the UKRAINE was given to the GERMANS for war reparation by Russia in the Treaty of Brest Litovsk. (Russia did this repeatedly in history whenever Russia would profit from it, for example the Treaty of Andrussovo).

Thus, the Germans occupied the entire Ukraine until the war ended in the West, from 1917 to 1919. Meanwhile, the Germans confiscated everything that was not "nailed down." Anna's crops were confiscated that year, the livestock was confiscated, the library was taken (including the shelving), and of course, Anna's collection of paintings was hauled off to Germany! So, overnight they changed from well to do KULAKS to paupers. In 1919, Germany capitulated and the German Wehrmacht left the Ukraine. But, this made a bad situation only worse, now Reds and Whites were roaming the countryside taking whatever they pleased, exerting their right from the barrel of a gun.

Then, in 1919, Bolshevik agitators poisoned the well, ruined the orchards and Anna, Gabriel and Emilia fled to Kharkiev. Then, in 1926, the Communists changed the capital from Kiyiv to Kharkiev, russified the Ukrainian DON and KUBAN, just like they did in 2014 in the Crimea, integrating them into "Mother Russia" as the remaining Ukraine tried to establish an independent state. In all, some nine foreign armies kept cris crossing the Ukraine, devastating the countryside as they would pass. So, from 1917 and until 1926 there was total chaos and mayhem in the Ukraine. Finally, in 1926, Anna and Gabriel were assessed "BACK TAXES" for the last 12 years. The taxes were more than the estate was worth. So, there was nothing else left but to abandon the estate. And, in this way all Kulaks in the Ukraine became disenfranchised.

Meanwhile, Emilia was tutored at home. When schools began to open in 1925, she took and passed her high school exam and got her high school diploma at the age of 12. Of course, at age 12 it was impossible to start at a University, so Emilia decided to go to an AGRICULTURAL college. The minimum age there was 14, so she lied about her age and got accepted.

By 16 she was a licensed agronomist. The agricultural college was a "hands on" college with about 500 students. There, the students learned not only the theory, but applied the theory with daily applications. A confiscated estate was used as a "live" model. The students were broken down into teams of 10 and alternated not only with the agricultural work but also with the daily chores. So, they seeded, planted, maintained the orchards, maintained the livestock, cooked, baked and cleaned the entire estate.

This schooling proved to be invaluable later on for Emilia. And, she acquired a habit, she would buy "en gross." That is, when she went out to buy some cabbage, she would bring home a truck full of cabbage and then make the "darndest" cabbage products which lasted us for an entire year. That is, sauerkraut, coleslaw, dried cabbage and much more.

Then, she turned her attention to a University and chose to take up medicine in ODESSA. At age 17, she met my father on the train from Odessa to Kharkiev and they got married. In 1930, she transferred to STALINO (my father worked near by) and she got her medical degree. In 1931, my older sister was born. At that time my father was the technical director of the chemical plant in ZINOVSK (now ELIZAVETOVGRAD) and Chief Chemist with 107 patents to his name.

In 1933, my father Ivan founded the Ukrainian Chemical Society (the picture is shown on the Internet). But, constant exposure to harmful gases made him deathly sick in 1935. As soon as my father got sick he was deprived of all his privileges, he was even "de listed" from the "International Who's Who." So, they moved to Kiyiv.

At that time the government was building out the suburbs of Kiyiv. In Kiyiv, Emilia took up MICROBIOLOGY and HYDROBIOLOGY while nursing my father back to health. In addition, she volunteered to teach Russian and Russian Literature at night (it was forbidden to speak or teach Ukrainian) for "underprivileged" students without pay. That is, teenagers, most of them orphans from the CIVIL WAR and WW I. And, if that was not enough, she decided to start a new project. To build herself a house. One that was nicer and more functional than the mansion in the estate. This was not a small undertaking, even under the best of circumstances. But, at that time this was a herculean task, for the Ukraine was denuded of all "HARDWARE and MASONRY" by the Germans, the Civil War and the unending requisitions by STALIN.

However, the new administration in Kiyiv was expanding the outskirts of Kiyiv and all workers were eligible for a parcel of land which they had to cultivate or improve. Since Emilia worked and my father was recuperating, she was eligible for two parcels. So, she went to the bureau and got herself two parcels in the KURINIV district in Kiyiv. Then, she went to the "forestry office" and got 100 cubic meters of timber, all seasoned oak, enough to built three mansions, not one. When it was pointed out to her that this was way too much timber for one house, she only smiled and in the end she got her way.

Next, the timber had to be lugged to a mill and the finished product lugged back to the building site. Here, she recruited her students. Emilia offered them a good wage but they had to bring a truck. Next day her entire class showed up with five "requisitioned" trucks and they hauled her timber to the mill. The mill charged her two sacks of flour for the job. Emilia delivered 3 sacks and got a perfect job in return. So, when

---

it was finished, her students came again and hauled the boards, beams and studs, back to the building site. Next, she had to find a carpenter and a mason to build her a full cellar, the foundation and the frame. In those days few people worked for money because the money was nearly worthless, but all wanted a finished product. So, Emilia found a carpenter, who agreed to build her the frame and do all the masonry work for 1/3 of her lumber! She agreed and, within two months she had a magnificent house with the largest cellar imaginable.

Then, she proceeded to "stock" the cellar. She would go to the market and buy cabbage, green tomatoes, cucumbers, peppers, olives, fruits, mushrooms, onions, garlic, practically all by the truckload. She bought a dozen or so wheel barrels and prepared them for use, which is no small task in itself. Then, she hired a few local women and proceeded to pickle, marinate and cook all these vegetables and fruits. Within a month, the cellar was stocked to the brim with finished products, sauerkraut, coleslaw, pickles, pickled tomatoes, marinated mushrooms, preserves, compotes and so on.

Once the cellar was stocked, she had a barn built; fenced the property and acquired a few farm animals, a few pigs, a flock of geese, chickens and the biggest and gentlest St. Bernard you can imagine, I called him FUZZY (loosely translated).

Finally, she planted an orchard of "ANTONOV APPLES" and two Pear trees. Then, along the fence she planted berry bushes, Gooseberries, Raspberries and many other varieties. Along her orchard, she planted strawberries and left herself a mini garden. The second parcel was used to grow wheat, barely and sunflowers.

However, while Emilia was on the "roll," one disaster after another hit the Ukraine and her family. First, in 1936 her brother NICK was arrested and sent to Siberia for 20 years, for being a student at the University. A student from that University was accused of having killed KIROV and the entire student body was arrested and exiled for 20 years to Siberia, with a loss of all human rights for 10 years. It took Emilia and her family two years to locate Nick and send him "care packages."

52

Then, in 1936, STALIN decided to collectivize all farms in the Ukraine. The farmers resisted and the worst genocide humanity has seen occurred in the Ukraine. The Soviet military was sent to the Ukraine, they cordoned off all access to all cities and proceeded to take away all grain, foodstuff and farm animals from the farmers. By 1939 over 10 million Ukrainians starved to death. Emilia was lucky in that most of her immediate members of her family had moved to the city. But, members of her extended family who remained in the countryside all perished during that time. The Ukraine was literally depopulated by Stalin, about 1/4 of the entire population in the Ukraine was starved to death this way! In the midst of this chaos, I was born, on November 1, 1937.

Then, in 1941 HITLER invaded the Soviet Union. The Ukraine saw Germany as a liberator and most Ukrainians preferred fighting with the Germans against STALIN. So, the huge Soviet army charged with the defense of KIYIV, with KHRUSHCHEV as the commissar, "disintegrated" before the Germans arrived. Kiyiv could not be defended, nor evacuated. So, KHRUSHCHEV issued orders to destroy the city and many historical buildings were leveled, including the 1000 year old PECHERSKA monastery. Then, he set up 100 execution squads or so and, unleashed them to kill all prominent citizens of KIYIV. On that list was my father. And a few days before the Germans entered KIYIV they ambushed my father and shot him. They did not kill him, but shot him so many times that he bled to death.

Neighbors rushed to his aid, but they were held back at gunpoint. Someone rushed to my mother's work place and told her what happened. Emilia rushed to the scene, and unafraid of their guns took her husband and rushed him to the nearest hospital, but, he was pronounced dead on arrival.

From then on, Emilia wowed not to live in a regime which did not value human life. She took me to the site where my father was murdered, and made me see the field where my father bled to death. And, she told me then and there, "A government which does not value her citizens does not deserve the loyalty of her citizens, there is only one country I know of, where I want to live from now on and that is: AMERICA."

When the Germans moved into Kiyiv they were welcomed with flowers, bread and salt. The newsreels are full of these pictures. But, within a few months the "German Masterrace" showed their teeth as soon as the administrators moved it. And, they were not pretty. In the beginning many Ukrainians went to Germany voluntarily. Soon that became a trickle. And now the Germans forced Ukrainians to go to Germany as slave labors in cattle cars. Resistance was slow in forming but it got stronger by the day.

Meanwhile our neighbors urged Emilia to take a job in the city administration. Emilia agreed and became the assistant to the Kuriniv Mayor Dr. Bagazil. During the German occupation she was arrested many times. But, each time her guardian angel would come to her rescue. In 1943, after the Battle of Kursk, it became obvious to many folks that the Germans would loose the war. So, Emilia secured a "MARSHBEFEHL" for herself and her children. And, according to Emilia, she left Kiyiv on the last train to Berlin.

I remember distinctly when we left Kiyiv, because my shoes were new and a bit tight, as I walked in the dew to "soften" them up; yet I watched my mother. When we left, Emilia never looked back, not once. The house she built, the orchard she planted, the few measly possessions she buried, they all meant nothing. Now, she and her children had to survive and make it to AMERICA.

And, after many tribulations, she achieved that goal also. Eventually, in 1957, we came to AMERICA despite the objections from George (her 2nd husband), Emma and me.

However, there were many tribulations to be overcome. First, we had to make it to Berlin. As we retreated, most of the time the Soviet army was no more than 50 miles behind us. If we were ever caught that would be the end of us. The KGB has a long, unforgiving memory. Then we had to survive the bombings. We were bombed out twice and once our bunker suffered a direct hit. From our family only George got hurt.

Then, came the Soviet occupation. Anyone who wanted to survive in Berlin had to trade with the Soviets. Many times Emilia risked her life so that her family could eat. In the end Emilia was caught by Smersh in Wustermark near Berlin. She was imprisoned, interrogated and beaten. But, she was released only because our neighbor was Dr. Derz, the leader of the SED, a left wing party in Berlin. As soon a Emilia was released she and George went to the English commandant, we lived in the British sector, who gave her and her family asylum.

Once in West Germany, Emilia and George had to undergo a "de nazification" program. American Intelligence was located in Southern Bavaria, in the Mittenwald Oberammergau area. By 1951 they were cleared by the Allied Intelligence and allowed to leave for Munich. By 1955, George and Emma got a job working for Radio Liberty. George became editor in the Russian section and Emma became an announcer in the Ukrainian section. While George and Emma were gainfully employed I landed the most lucrative "Stamp Business" you could imagine (see the section on Stamps).

Then, in 1957 the KGB nearly caught George in the center of Munich. A taxi pulled up next to George; two men jumped out and tried to drag George into their cab. While George resisted the best he could he also screamed for help at the top of his voice. Instantly many came to his aid and freed him. An exasperated George arrived home and told Emilia. Emilia called for a taxi, and with George in tow went immediately to the American consulate. There, they asked for political asylum and got it. Emilia also requested to immigrate to America. They filled out the necessary applications and within a few days they received word that they were accepted as immigrants to America. They sold most of their possessions and crated the rest, destination USA.

Each one of us was allowed a crate for our personal property. I sold some stamps, in order to have some cash on hand, about $1,000, and crated the rest, including other books and papers. And, since the headquarters of Radio Liberty was in New York City, George was effectively transferred to New York City.

Emma effectively took leave and had to return within a year. As soon as we entered New York City (right at the airport), we applied for American citizenship, which takes five years before one is actually eligible for citizenship. Since there were no wars of any kind, I was allowed to claim a student exemption. That is, my draft status became 2S. Which meant that by September 15, I had to be enrolled in an accredited college or go serve in the army.

Welcome to America, and meet the first scam! In those days when we arrived in America, it was still mandatory for all newcomers to have a sponsor. Since we left in such a great hurry we could not get a regular sponsor. However, there was a "Russian Foundation" called "The Tolstoy Foundation" which sprung into action whenever unsuspecting "Russians" arrived in America. Since George had declared himself to be a Russian, it was presumed that the entire family was Russian. Well, it was not so, not by a long shot. Emma was a staunch Ukrainian and would not be caught dead to be called a Russian. I was educated in Germany, so to me German was my affiliation. Emilia was either way, Ukrainian or Russian and Kathy did not count.

We came to America with the "Flying Tiger Line." They did not fly a regular route. We left from Munich Riem to London, from London to Keflavick (Iceland), from Keflavick to Goose Bay (Canada). Midway our plane developed engine problems and we were handed a flashlight, a life jacket and shark repellant. As it was March, and glancing at the route of our plane, we would not last two minutes in the water without turning to icicles.

The Flying Tiger Line was not a regular airline. Therefore, we had to land someplace in New Jersey. However, when we arrived, an official from the Tolstoy Foundation was waiting for us, with a huge sign for all to see.

We spotted him and we introduced ourselves. He took us to the "Hudson Terminal," still in New Jersey. And, once we crossed the Hudson in a ferry, we were in Manhattan. From there we took a cab to Pennsylvania Station. From there we took a bus to Valley Stream, the center of the Tolstoy Foundation, in the middle of nowhere in New Jersey. Then, we were taken to a bungalow and told the "House Rules." Room and board was $10.00 per day per person. No cooking and no pets.

In 1957, that was an enormous amount of money for five people. But, the first night nobody complained. We were just plain ecstatic to be in America.

As soon as we settled in, Emilia and George went shopping to investigate the food situation. They came back complaining that everything was so expensive. And, now Emilia started to have second thoughts about our expenses. Our family had five members. At $10.00 per day per person that translated to $1,500.00 a month; that is $18,000.00 per year. George's monthly pay was not much more than that, but he had to pay for transportation and incidentals; never mind the family expenses. It was one thing to stay there a few days or even a month, but to stay there any length of time was not for Emilia.

Next day Emilia took action. As soon as everybody was up and ready for breakfast she announced to all: "Get me a New York City telephone book. I will find someone I know, who will help us." To all of us, this seemed like the most ridiculous exercise. How in the world could Emilia find here someone she knew? But obediently we started to look for a phone book and we found one.

As soon as we got her the book, she opened it and thought for a while. Then she would zero in on a letter and search. By the time she reached the third letter "R" she found a "hit." All we heard was, "I found him!"

Indeed, she found a good friend from Kiyiv no less: Nick Rodalitzky. Nick was a broker and had a real estate office in Manhattan! She called Nick and he promised to come and see us the next day.

The next morning Nick arrived. First, everybody had to sit down and catch up on the news. Then, we had to explain how we got into this mess. Finally, Nick told Emilia he had the right solution for our situation. A four bedroom apartment in a good district (Washington Heights), and only $80.00 per month. But, there was a "catch." The building (255 Haven Avenue) was scheduled to be demolished within four years, with two years of guaranteed stay. Nick assured Emilia that within a year he would have another apartment ready for us in a better neighborhood at a similar price. What was important now was to get out of the clutches of the Tolstoy Foundation.

Why is it that most scams a perpetrated on the most unsuspecting and needy people. Nick saved us from a financial calamity.

Once we settled in Haven Avenue I had very little to do. I decided to "explore New York City." We lived right near the George Washington Bridge. That is, right at 181st Street. I decided to walk the length of Manhattan island. So, the first day I started to walk along the Hudson River. Apparently nobody ever walks along the Hudson river, because for long stretches there are no sidewalks and no "shoulder" to walk on. Thus, before I reached Battery Park cops stopped me at least a dozen times. But I made it despite of them.

Next day I walked down Broadway. This time, the cops did not bother me at all and I began to get a great perspective of New York City. Then, I walked down a few more Avenues. Each time when I reached Battery Park I would explore the neighborhood and then take the subway home. In the end, I had to explore the "Village." Then, I would take the A Train to 14th Street and walk every street from West to East, then move down one street and walk it from East to West. I would repeat that until I reached Houston Street. Then, I would explore "Chinatown and Little Italy." My last section was Wall Street. Once that was done, I knew Manhattan like the "Palm of my hand."

Within 10 days I knew New York City better than any "native." Next, I would explore specific sections. On one such trip I decided to explore the "Columbia University Area" on 116th Street and beyond. I took the A Train to 116th Street, bought myself three papers, the New York Times, the "Hoboe News," a Russian paper and a German paper. Then, I found a bench and started reading them, flipping from one to the other.

I sat there for about 20 minutes when a young man started talking to me: "Do you read all three papers," I heard. When I replied in the positive, he continued: "Don't mind me, but I am a graduate student from Columbia and in order to get my Masters I must choose a foreign language. Would you help me with Russian?"

This was music to my ears. I replied, "Gladly, if you help me also." He asked how he can help. Now, I told him my story; that I was "just off the boat" and I needed to find a College by September 15th which would accept me. He was "ready, willing and able" to introduce me to his advisor in the Engineering School of Columbia, Dr. Pashkish, who happened to be German. So, we introduced one another and we set up a schedule for him and an appointment for me. His name was Stan and I introduced myself as Anatoly.

At home I put all my report cards together and went to the appointment. Stan took me to his advisor and introduced me. I explained my situation (in German) and gave him my report cards. I could see he was thinking and thinking and then he finally got it, and turned to me:" My recommendation is you go to a small school. One that is associated with Columbia. You enter a "pre engineering" program with them and after the third year you transfer to Columbia and in two years you will get two degrees at once, a BS and an MS from Columbia in Engineering. Meanwhile you will see a little of America. What do you think?" I was delighted, I said: "Yes, by all means." Once I agreed, he picked up his phone and called a number. Then I heard, "Dean Winters please." After a pause, "Hi, this is Pashkish, I have this foreign student here in my office. Will you talk to him on your next visit?" The rest I could not make out...

When he finished, he turned to me and said: "On his next trip to New York City he will talk to you. He will come here on a recruitment drive. He is the Dean of Franklin and Marshall College in Lancaster Pennsylvania, Amish country... you will like it. If it does not turn out, come and see me again."

I was jubilant, my greatest hurdle had been overcome. I waited anxiously for the appointed day. And, when I met Dean Winters I had a great meeting with him, even though my English was not the best, and I noticed him smiling many times. We ended the meeting with, "You must come to F & M and meet with Mr. Russell, he teaches Freshmen English. He is blind, from childhood. But he graduated from Oxford and was a top notch wrestler in the United States." Thus, a date was set and I promised to be there.

On the appointed day I took the train to Lancaster, Pa. The College was only a short walk away. I went straight to Dean Winters' office. When I arrived Dean Winters came to meet me right away. Then, together we walked to the English Department Building. There, the Dean pointed me in the direction and said, "The last door to your left."

I was racking my brains, how to properly address this professor. I came to the door, I knocked and I heard, "Come in."

I walked in, walked up to the desk and I heard, "Please, be seated. Your name?" I mustered my best Shakespearean English and blurted out, "My name is Anatoly Kandiew, how ar'est thou?" The man nearly fell off his chair, I had made an impression alright but I was not quite sure whether it was the desired one. The rest of our interview was uneventful. In the end, I was accepted by the College.

When the semester started I was eager to sign up. I signed up for mostly upperclassmen courses in Physics, Organic Chemistry and Calculus in Mathematics, Religion and Freshmen English. Then, Dean Winters came to me and looked at my schedule, "My, what a schedule," he said. I replied, "Actually, I would like to take up Philosophy, that interests me the most." The Dean looked at me, "Why don't you? Who's stopping you?" I replied, "My English is bad and I am afraid to take all English type courses." The Dean looked at me and said, "That is nonsense, take what you prefer, then you will excel." Elated, I went and re registered loading up with "Humanities." That day I wrote a letter to Emilia, my mother, "How the Dean helped me select the courses I wished to take."

I few days went by when I received a Telephone call. It was Emilia. Then I heard, "What have you done? I have two Philosophers at home already, I do not need a third one?

Therefore, you either change your program to science or you come home." Greatly disappointed, I agreed to change my program to "science," that is, Mathematics.

In retrospect, Emilia was right. I graduated in 3 years in Mathematics and ended up in the Computer Field. What a fabulous decision Emilia forced on me...

Once my College situation was secured I tried to find work until September. I would respond to classified adds especially by engineering firms. But in every case the story was the same; my English was inadequate and everyone knew I would be only a short time employee. Then, one day, George suggested to contact a Russian Orthodox priest,

Alexander Kiselev, who ran a children camp in the summer in the Catskill Mountains, a resort area known also as the "Borscht Belt."

I went to see the priest with all the credentials I could muster. In Germany I was a Boy Scout and I had risen to "Jungfeldmeister," the equivalent of Junior Scout Master. I was permitted to run a camp for Boy Scouts and so on. Once I showed him my papers he hired me on the spot. I was put in charge of the boys camp. (The girls camp had their own leader). We agreed on a fixed price for June through August. It was just enough money to pay for my tuition. Emilia promised to pay for my incidentals and for room and board. So, my first year was taken care of.

This left me some time from April to May. It so happened that in May, Alexander ran an "Ecumenical" camp for teenagers and I was invited to attend for free. In addition, the campsites needed to be prepared and cleaned up. This, he scheduled for April. So my calendar was full, and I went with him at the first opportunity to his place called "Accord Farms." During the last days of May we had to pick up the children for the camp. So, we returned to New York, loaded up the kids in a big bus and dove them to the "Farm." On that trip I met my future girlfriend and wife.

When I graduated from Franklin and Marshall in 1960, I had two choices; accept an assistantship at Storrs (UCON) or Maryland or get married and start my career. I debated long and hard, but the prospect to remain on Emilia's purse strings did not appeal to me and the assistantship did not pay enough to be "independent." So, I decided to get married. Emilia had never met my girlfriend's parents. (She met my girlfriend at my graduation. She was there with her "Uncle," Constantine).

Every summer, starting in June my girlfriend's family went on a vacation. Her father was George, who was a Chemist. He worked at Merk's in New Jersey. He was a highly educated man and a Ukrainian at heart, but he was totally hen pecked by his wife Vera. Vera was not educated at all, and worked at Regina, assembling cleaners and sweepers. The uncle was even less educated. He worked for a "cable" company rolling cable onto huge wooden "rollers," used by AT&T.

That year they had picked a spot in Maine, near Augusta and I decided to take Emilia and Kathy there to meet them in an "as casual setting" as possible. They preferred a "pension." That is, a place that offered room and board. Board, meant breakfast and dinner. For lunch they would prepare sandwiches we could take with us on a trip or excursion. The food was claimed to be exceptional. We picked a date, made reservations and drove down to Maine. They drove down in their car and I loaded up Emilia and Kathy in my red Plymouth Convertible and we were on our way (in my pimp mobile).

The fellow who ran the pension, Pisarevsky by name, was a "real Cossack." He was a Ukrainian through and through and Emilia made instant friends with him. He had his own "smoke house," and bought lobsters by the crate. Their meals were fabulous and everybody was enjoying themselves. Then, one day Emilia pulled me aside and said, "Tolja, I have to talk to you."

I knew something unpleasant awaited me. I came up to her and said, "Nu." Emilia put her hand on my shoulder and led me to a deserted place. She started: "Do you know what you got yourself into?" Before I could answer she continued, "I have made friends with Pisarevsky. He is such a great guy. The stories he told me, I would not believe. Do you know they have been coming here for a few years? Do you know they go though the same routine every year? They take two rooms, one for George and Vera and the other for Constantine. Then, at midnight, every night, Vera goes, with a lit candle in hand, to Constantine. She stays in his room all night. Then, just before dawn she comes out, with a lit candle in hand, and returns to her room. They have been lovers for over 20 years. Pisarevsky got this from George. The only reason they stay together is because of the girls. And, your future bride is 18!"

"So what,..." I said "I am not marrying Vera, I plan to marry her daughter." She just looked at me in disbelief. Then she continued, "I did not believe Pisarevsky at first. So, at night, just before midnight, I watched the whole story myself. I tell you, what Pisarevsky knows, all world knows. You will be made a sucker, just like George." To this I replied, "This will never happen." She thought for a while and said, "Life is hard enough in its own way. It is sad you will have to look over your shoulder all your life because the apple does not fall far from the apple tree. But let me tell you this, should you go ahead and marry her I will give you and her all my support and blessings." Then, she continued: "What about a dowry?" I replied: "I don't expect a dowry." She just looked at me and said: "Too bad. As you can see, they were "parasites then, and they are parasites now!" They try to steal the benefits of your education for her!"

As it turned out Emilia was right. We got married and eventually we had a very bitter divorce.

Eventually Emilia got also a divorce. After she reached financial independence, George decided to have a "last fling" with a 19 year old, called Lila. Emilia split the assets, George wanted to split only the cash. He felt anything with a "mortgage" on it, was a capitalist trap.

Right after Emilia's divorce she went to Europe to visit Emma. (Emma was still working at Radio Liberty). On her return home, Emilia took a cab home from the airport. As she was approaching home, a terrible thunderstorm developed. Then, a thunderclap scared the taxi driver who jumped the curb and hit a fire hydrant. Emilia was badly hurt and was hospitalized. When she was released she started to have "eye problems."

Her doctor send her to "Manhattan Eye and Ear" where they performed an eye operation and told her to come back in three months. Again, she had to undergo another eye operation and they told her to come back in three months again.

This time Emilia went to her doctor and asked what other alternatives were available to her. He thought for a while and then he said: "You know, there is a lake in Florida, called Warm Mineral Springs, it has some unexplained healing powers. Go there, see if the waters help you."

That is all Emilia had to hear. Next day she was packed, went to Pennsylvania Station, and was on her way to Florida. At the lake was a Real Estate Office which also rented out homes for practically any length of time. So, she rented a house for three months and started to go to the lake every day for her entire stay. When she arrived at the lake the first time, she felt at home right away. To her it was a "regular KALYBAN." People walked around, breast deep in water and sang. And, they sang in UKRAINIAN. She felt right at home. (Actually, the lake was in shape of a crater with the deep part roped off. The total diameter was about 100 yards with a run off at one end).

When her three months were up she packed her stuff and took the airplane back to New York. She went to her eye appointment. They looked at her every which way but did not operate. After they were all done, the leading doctor came to her and said: "I don't know what you have done, but your "detached retina" seems to be heeling by itself. Why don't you continue doing what you were doing and come back in three months."

This was music to Emilia's ears. She sold or put on the market all her properties in New York. She hired a person with a truck and moved to Florida. With plenty of cash in hand she started to deal in properties and homes. She had a wonderful time as she traded right "in the lake," the properties and homes. All her relatives in New York got a "standing invitation" to come and visit her. Needless to say all relatives and family members visited her on a regular basis. But, no paradise lasts forever.

At one point Emilia fell off her motorized tricycle. In the fall she hurt her breast. She went to the doctor with me in tow.

The doctor recommended to do a biopsy, to find out if her swelling was cancerous. She agreed. It was specifically agreed that the doctor do only a biopsy, nothing else. I was in the waiting room waiting for the results. Next thing I know, her doctor came in and announced, "That he had performed a mastectomy." I was outraged. (Just because she had excellent insurance, the doctor mutilated her. These doctors are typically called "New York Flunkies" here. They come to Florida, rip off their patients and then hide themselves in a veil doctor immunity).

But for the time being there was nothing else to do but to have her admitted to the hospital. When Emilia came out of sedation I told her what happened and urged her to find an attorney and sue the doctor and the hospital. But, Emilia would not hear of it. That operation destroyed her life. (As it turned out the doctor OD'd and died shortly thereafter).

When I got my second divorce, I planned to go to the West Coast to use my skills there. As far as I was concerned Florida had no jobs in my field, in quantitative analysis. But Emilia asked me to join her, and I decided to stay with Emilia.

The next few years were terrific. I am an opera buff. So I would get from our library: Operas, Operettas, Musicals and many great films she had not seen. During the day we explored, I would take her to the mall, or beach or drive around and explore the neighborhood. At that time, Gorbachev bought himself a villa on Gasperilla Island, which was not too far from us. When we returned, we would have dinner and then it was "Showtime!"

Emilia died August 27, 2001. A few days before 9/11. She wanted to be cremated which I arranged, and I buried her in Deerfield Beach, in a cemetery in the "PIONEER PARK" of all places. To Emilia this would have been the ultimate resting place, since in "her" Russia the Pioneers were a youth movement. With the standard joke: "From the back a pioneer, from the front a pensioner." But, in all fairness, Emilia had become a true American.

The Candybombers

On June 24, 1948, Sir Winston Churchill started the "Cold War" with the Soviet Union with his infamous "Iron Curtain Speech" in Fulton College in America.

After that, the political situation was rapidly deteriorating between the Western allies and the Soviets. Stalin was determined to exercise his reparation concessions from his Western allies. Most important on his mind was territory as a means of reparation.

The new borders with Finland, Poland, and the Baltic coast were firmly integrated into to the Soviet Union. East Prussia and Pommerania were his main prize for German reparations. For his declaration of war on Japan and the conquest of Manchuria, he was free to grab the south of Sakhalin Island and the Kuril islands. This he did, and parts of China were conveniently integrated into the Soviet Union.

The puppet governments in Albania, Bulgaria, Czechoslovakia, Hungary, Jugoslavia, Poland and Rumania were firmly in Stalin's hands. Then, he extricated additional pieces from Italy, Germany and Austria. East Germany was an obedient slave to Stalin. Only one isolated spot remained free within East Germany: Berlin.

Then, Berlin was singled out to be economically "strangled" by the Soviets in retaliation. It took them nearly two years to come up with a proper Soviet response, apply brute force to win an advantage. This was always the means of Soviet or Russian expansion. They closed all access roads to Berlin and planned to starve the Berliners, to teach the West a lesson.

As always, Russia or her rulers know only one way to rule: by terror. This method they acquired from the Tartars, who ruled Moscow from 1240 to 1610. Ultimately, Catherine II, the German adventurist, conquered the last remaining Tartar Khanate in the Crimea in 1787.

Most of the time the Ukraine was singled out. Moscow started out as a tiny enclave. But, with the help from the Tartars, Moscow expanded at the expense of the Ukraine. The most recent "terror grabbing" occurred in 2014 with the annexation of the Ukrainian Crimea. I have a solution for the Ukraine to recover the Crimea and the prior land grabs of 1926 of the Don and the Kuban. All the Ukraine has to do is to become Catholic. Then, all of Europe will be dedicated in restoring all prior Ukrainian lands. Besides, a small portion of the Ukraine is Catholic already. And Orthodoxy posed only grief, disillusionment and betrayal by the Muscovites.

The other aspect of war reparation included the dismantling of entire factories and industrial complexes. So, East Germany and Berlin were systematically raped of their remaining industries for war reparations. Finally, there was the human toll: All former Soviet citizens were subject to forced repatriation.

Berlin was fighting a bottomless "black hole." As soon as an industry was created or repaired, it was dismantled and shipped to the Soviet Union. Starvation rations kept the population chronically undernourished and unfit for hard labor. Stalin's attempt to convert the Berliners to farmers was essentially a dismal failure. The small patches of land were plundered before the crop was ready. Berlin needed food. That food had to come from West Germany.

While Berlin has many canals, most of them lead to East Germany; and East Germany was essentially in the same predicament as Berlin, no factories, no work and no food. The only main arteries from Berlin to West Germany were roads. In fact, three main roads connect Berlin to West Germany: One to Hamburg, the other to Hannover, and the last to 'Frankfurt am Main.' This was the 'Autobahn;' which Hitler had built.

Stalin saw an opportunity to strangle Berlin, to cut off all supplies from the West. This, he hoped, would force the western allies to abandon

Berlin. Then, East Germany would be "homogeneous." The "corrupt" western influence would be eliminated.

First, Stalin tried political means to win over the Berliners. They were promised larger rations and better working conditions if they voted for the SED in the combined Berlin election of 1946. The SED was soundly defeated. To the Berliners, the Americans, the English, and the French were their last glimmer of hope. There was no way Berliners would vote away their presence. Each Soviet attempt to front another Communist party was defeated. What remained was an annexation by force.

Of course, a pretext needed to be found. That pretext was right at hand. Even though Churchill's speech was the obvious pretext, another pretext, more acceptable to World Communism needed to be propagandized. West Germany had just instituted its final currency reform. The "Deutsche Mark (D Mark)" was created and the provisional currency was replaced. This pretext was used by Stalin to begin the blockade in June of 1948. His explanation to the allied powers was simple: The new currency reform undermined the currency in East Germany.

Fortunately for Berlin, the Allies did not see it that way. They recognized the act for what it was, another way for Stalin to wrestle more territory from the West. The Allies responded swiftly. An airlift was created to supply Berlin with much needed food and fuel.

That is, Americans came to the rescue with an all out airlift flying in everything needed for the Berliner's survival; food, coal, medicine and so on.

When the blockade began, the Berliners trembled at the possibility of another war. Was Hitler's assumption right? Could Communism and Capitalism not coexist? Was war the only inevitable solution?

At any rate, it can be said that the actual cold war between East and West began with the blockade of Berlin on June 1948. To the youngsters of Berlin, this was a "miracle." And it became practically a sacred duty to go to Tempelhof Airport and watch the American armada fly in the supplies. American pilots spotted the boys and girls lined up on their flight path and almost from the beginning the pilots started to drop little parachutes with a variety of candy, chewing gum and small chocolate bars in them. This was truly a miracle. I don't recall seeing a chocolate bar until then, never mind having one!

The situation in Berlin now deteriorated quickly. No more joint patrols. No more collaboration with the Soviets for forceful repatriation. An actual border was established between East and West Berlin. Barbed wire was strung between East and West Berlin. (Only much later, during President Kennedy's term, was the infamous wall erected). Berliners took to the streets and demonstrated, and "Checkpoint Charlie" was created at the Brandenburg Gate.

I remember how, on the first day of the airlift, I listened to my radio all day long. The tension continued for the next few days as I listened intently. Allegedly, the first few flights were "buzzed" by MIG's. But, no incidents occurred to provoke a shooting war. Within a few weeks, the airlift became routine. Just another inconvenience for the Berliners to deal with. Special taxes were imposed to pay for the airlift. The tax was paid not only in Berlin, but also in West Germany.

When the Berlin Airlift began in 1948, our gang (kids from our street) decided to make the pilgrimage to Tempelhof Airport, watch the candy bombers and collect their "droppings." When we arrived, there was a huge mob of kids. They had positioned themselves along the flight path and stood their ground. Sure enough each time a plane approached, it unloaded a heap of little parachutes all along their flight path. Thousands upon thousands (so it seemed) of little parachutes were slowly drifting to the ground, and the kids would break their cluster and dash toward a parachute. Amazingly, there were so many parachutes that each kid got at least one.

Still, for me it was an ordeal to go to Tempelhof, and I went only once. I would not tell my mother about it for fear that I would be grounded for a month or so. Basically, I was not allowed to stray too far from our residence. But, let me tell you, the candy bombers were a big hit in Berlin...

Eventually, word got to the kids in East Berlin. They wrote letters to the "Candy Bombers" begging them to fly by in East Berlin. And, believe it or not, after some intense negotiations with the Soviets, the Americans were allowed to fly over the East Sector of Berlin and shower the kids with "bombs."

Very few people know about the lovable and heroic Candy Bombers. In my opinion this is very sad. They should be applauded, praised and advertized to the whole world. Let me assure you that to the Berliners, they will be remembered forever or as long as Berlin exists...

With the airlift, the rations improved. Many products could now be bought in the stores. The black market began to disappear. The airlift lasted until September 1949. It is said that the airlift cost nearly two hundred million dollars. In 1949, that was a tidy sum.

Because of the airlift, approximately two million West Berliners were saved. Also because of the airlift, Berlin became the refuge for most refugees from East Berlin, East Germany and Eastern Europe. Berlin became the showcase of the West and a nagging eyesore for the East.

While exact figures are not available, the following estimates can be made:

In 1941, Berlin had a population in excess of 4.5 million inhabitants. As the Soviets came closer to Berlin, more than 2 million refugees flooded into the city. Let us say that 6.5 million people were in Berlin at the end of the war in 1945. Of these, fewer than 1 million were killed during the bombings and the subsequent battle for Berlin. This left 5.5 million inhabitants at the end of the war in Berlin.

A 1959 census revealed 2.2 million West Berliners and 1.1 million East Berliners were left, or a total of 3.3 million Berliners. Let us say that the "exodus" from Berlin, which was a trickle until 1949, and the natural birthrate cancelled each other out. Then, the starvation of Berlin killed approximately 3.2 million people. This starvation was deliberate and planned. This starvation was masterminded by Stalin.

Eventually, Stalin took his venom even further. It can be said that the Korean War was the final offshoot of Churchill's speech and provocation of Stalin. What a price to pay to vent one's displeasure...

Bubus Americanus

Here we are at war again (IRAQ) yet practically everybody in America pretends that everything is normal. Wars are expensive, who will pay for this war? Most likely you and me. Most likely the money in the Social Security trust fund will be the first to go. Why? Because it is READY MONEY, 1.3 trillion of it. This Money is to our politicians like a ripe fruit ready to be picked because it "hangs out there" in limbo, in a trust fund. But, when the Baby Boomers start retiring, Social Security will be in deep trouble because every penny of it will be needed to offset the cash intake for the next 10 to 15 years!

The cost of our war will be roughly 5 to 10 billion each month or 60 to 120 billion each year. So, by the time the Baby Boomers begin to retire, over the next 8 to 12 years, that trust fund will be depleted. And, then what? Who will lend us a few trillion dollars??? Our good friends? Great Britain, Germany or Japan? Not likely. Great Britain is nearly bankrupt now. Her Pound Sterling has declined from $4.80 to the US Dollar to $1.41. That is, the purchasing power of the once mighty Pound Sterling has declined 300%. Concurrently, once the sun never set on the British Empire. Today, she is left with a few "godforsaken rocks" which serve no purpose whatsoever. In fact they are only a drain on Great Britain. For example: Falkland Islands. Great Britain would be much better off gifting them to Argentina, but instead they made war over them!!!

Once the British travelled to INDIA in "POSH" style (Port Out, Starboard Home). But India wrestled her independence from Great Britain, and the great avalanche began. All nations in her empire clamored for independence, from large nations like India and Australia to Banana Republics like British Honduras and Bermuda. And the disintegration continues...

Even the GERMAN economic miracle has turned into inflation today. The acquisition of East Germany added a 10 million labor pool to the German economic machine. But, that labor pool is useless, it knows only government subsidies. Fifty years of COMMUNISM atrophied their drive, prudence and initiative. Now they expect only government handouts! So, the current generation has been written off and GERMANY is banking on the next generation to restore the proper work ethics!

Of course, the greatness of Great Britain was at the expense of Germany after World War I, when Great Britain and France mutilated Germany's Empire and gorged themselves at her expense. The reparations payments of World War I slapped on Germany, drove her into the great hyper inflation, which in turn drove her into poverty and made the rise of Hitler possible. Within two years, a 5 Mark postage stamp turned into a 50 Billion Mark stamp. Towards the end, workers were paid twice each day, for otherwise the earned wages were useless!!!

Hitler stopped the reparation payments, with the help of America and the Germans started to recover. But, the "reparations corporation" which was chartered to collect the reparation money was not abandoned, it still exists, and it adds each year a few trillion marks of "monopoly money" to its income ledger. So, aside from the current problems of integrating East Germany into her economy, Germany lives under the shadow of massive potential debt...

World War II was different, for once, we did not relinquish the peace terms to our allies, and instead of imposing additional reparations, America initiated the MARSHALL PLAN. Instead of wringing out a few 1000 trillions from GERMANY we made a trillion or so available to (mostly) Germany to rebuild her economy! And that's why the GERMAN economic miracle happened. Thus, Germany ended up with modern plants and equipment, while Great Britain was left to compete with outmoded factories and equipment. Naturally, whenever Germany sold against Great Britain it was no contest. So, the German economic miracle was at the expense of Great Britain, France, Italy and Spain. Therefore, it is not surprising that Germany became the economic leader in Europe and now wants to reconstruct the "HOLY ROMAN EMPIRE" under her leadership again, but along Hitler's guidelines. And, with the acceptance of the EURO, Germany seems to be succeeding...

We should remember the evolution of Germany's expansion. In the beginning Western Europe was Rome, which expanded into Gaul and into the Balkans. Along the Rhine River they build the "Limes" to keep the barbarian Germans out, and in the Balkans they built a "Limes" to keep the barbarian Goths out. Thus, it included today's Italy, France, Spain, Portugal; Croatia, Slovenia, Albania, Macedonia, Bulgaria and Greece.

The first expansion was with Charlemagne, he conquered Germany (between the Rhine and the Elbe Rivers) and set up a "Mark" on the right bank of the Elbe River displacing the Gothic Jutes, Angles, Sassons and the Wends. Then, when the Crusaders came home they needed something to do. So, the Pope organized them into the Order of Teutonic Knights and directed them to conquer the East for the Catholic Church. But that order was defeated at Tannenberg by a Lithuanian Duke (Vitus) who made them sign a treaty in which they agreed not to expand beyond the Vistula River.

Of course the Grandmaster of the Teutonic Order rushed speedily to Rome and lamented to the Pope how he had to abandon the conquest of the East at Tannenberg. The Pope did not think that much of the treaty. He told the Grandmaster to reorganize his men into a new order called the "Knights of the Sword" and continue the conquest, since there was no treaty against the new order. But, that new order failed to conquer the East.

Then came Napoleon; he expanded Western Europe to the Niemen River. This included Poland, because Maria Walevska had become his mistress and got pregnant by him. She bore him a son, but Napoleon would not acknowledge him (but took good care of his son and Maria), instead Napoleon realized that he could build a "Dynasty." Therefore, he divorced Josephine, resurrected the Pope and the Hapsburg Emperor and married Marie Louise, establishing a dynasty. But, when he demanded the "batan" to protect the Pope (that is, a change in the German Concordat), the Pope told him to go and conquer Russia. That became the end of Napoleon.

Then came Hitler. He too wanted a Concordat, in order to retain the loyalty of the Catholic Germans. Again, his request was granted, provided he conquer Russia. Thus, Hitler invaded the Soviet Union in 1941 with more than 6 million men (counting Germans and axis allies). The first setback happened at Moscow where Army Group North lost 95% of their motorized equipment, including tanks). In 1942, while Stalin thought Hitler would renew his attack on Moscow, Hitler struck in the Southern Ukraine. The goal was to capture the oil fields of Georgia and to capture Baku. The 6th Army (about 15 divisions, led by Paulus) was used to protect the flank of the main Army of Kleist. But the 6th Army was isolated and annihilated. Thus, Army Group South was destroyed.

In 1943, a huge bulge developed around Kursk. Hitler was ready to sue for peace. Molotow and von Ribbentropp met to discuss peace and the new fixed border. Hitler was satisfied keeping the "status quo," while Stalin demanded the old "Polish Border" of 1939. Thus, they could not agree on the territory and agreed that the battle of Kursk should decide the outcome. In the Battle of Kursk the Soviet Union had the advantage in arms (T/34's) and soldiers for the first time since the German offensive. And, Germany lost decisively in the middle of the summer.

After the Battle of Kursk, Germany was not able to launch another major offensive in the East. However, the claim for a new border for Western Europe was made, and the new European Union is making that claim. They already have admitted Estonia, Latvia and Lithuania into the European Union. The Ukraine has applied to be admitted and Byelorussia is watching the results.

Therefore, you can see that Putin is using the last possible terror tactic to prevent the Ukraine from joining the European Union. In my opinion, the Ukraine can reverse (and even gain some lost territory, like the Don and Kuban which they lost in 1926) if they simply convert to

Catholicism. The Ukraine has already many Catholics, and Orthodoxy has caused nothing but grief for the Ukraine!

The story in Japan was similar to Germany. America provided a trillion or so to rebuild Japan's economy. Mc Arthur used the "poker player" analogy and Japan was on her way to become again an economic superpower.

The upshot is that it is economically more advantageous to be America's enemy than ally. Peter Sellers made a movie about that. The premise is simple. Declare war on the United States, make war, surrender and then claim reconstruction money to line your pockets!

How quickly have we forgotten that Great Britain operates from an entirely different perspective. It is called GEOPOLITICS. The intellectual problem is simple: How can a small island nation exert her economic superiority among much larger nations. To this end Great Britain needed to identify her economic enemies first. And, they are: America, Russia, India, Africa and China.

Now, Cecil Rhodes, "developed Africa" for Great Britain, this was to be the great pool of "black gold." The pool of slaves Great Britain was to supply to the rest of the world! She even fought a war over it in Europe, and in the treaty of UTRECHT she gained the rights to be a monopoly in the slave trade!!! Thus, Africa was no longer an enemy but a resource.

Robert Clive, defeated the last Indian resistance in the battle of Plassy (1757), and India became part of the British Empire. Indians were to be used as KULIS world wide for the great industrial projects i.e. Panama canal, Suez canal etc., and as cannon fodder for the British wars to come (Crimea, World War I, and World War II). [There are more Indian graves at Monte Cassino, Italy, than any other nationality!] Thus, India became a resource rather than an enemy.

When China refused to trade with the British, opium was brought in and clandestine merchants quickly converted a nation of hard working Chinese into opium addicts. It can be said that Great Britain was the first nation to destroy the moral fiber of a country with the illicit drug trade. When China resisted, Great Britain launched the FIRST OPIUM WAR in 1838 which lasted to 1842. In the end, China was finished and Chinese kulis were exported to industrial projects, i.e. building the railroad tracks in America. Thus, while the Chinese bled to death, the British profited handsomely...

This left, America and Russia. These two enemies had to be encircled to contain their influence and competition.

To contain Russia, she needed to be denied access to the SEA. (Russia has no warm water port). To this end, Germany needed to be kept "relatively strong" to prevent Russia's expansion to the WEST. Gibraltar, Malta and Cyprus (and Egypt) would deny Russia the access to the MEDITERRANEAN. With INDIA under British rule the access to the SOUTH was blocked. This left the EAST wide open. Therefore, Japan needed to be groomed to prevent Russia's expansion to the EAST. And, by the end of the 19th century Japan became a devout ally of Britain. And, in 1905, Japan gave Russia a lesson in British military training and tactics. Thus, Russia was effectively encircled.

This left America to be taken care of. Here, Japan would play a double role and prevent America's expansion or trade to the West; Canada, the expansion or trade to the North; Mexico, the expansion or trade to the SOUTH. And, Great Britain would prevent America's expansion or trade to the EAST. Thus, America was effectively encircled also. The up shot was "The great depression in AMERICA." For the most part the result of this encirclement resulted in the great depression. Even though we call it as being due to "OUR ISOLATIONIST" policy at that time, close examination will clearly show that it was due to the economic encirclement, rather than to isolation. However, the encirclement policy is now politically incorrect. And, our historians have swallowed this hook, line and sinker.

During World War I, America lend billions of dollars to both Great Britain and France. And, while Great Britain and France enriched themselves at the expense of Germany, THE AMERICAN DEBT WAS NEVER REPAID. During World War II, America subsidized Great

Britain with billions of dollars, and to this date, THE AMERICAN DEBT HAS NOT BEEN REPAID.

So, while Great Britain has been riding out her storms with American money she coined a name for the American generosity: BUBUS AMERICANUS.

Sir Arthur Conan Doyle, sowed the initial seed in his story of Sherlock Homes. Who has not read his stories? Are they not "delightful?" Yet, the "bumbling idiot" in most of his stories is an AMERICAN who prevents the capture of the arch villain: MORIARITY. At the same time, we practically revere Sir ISAAC NEWTON, even though he was the greatest plagiarist the world has seen. He stole from: Archimedes, Galileo, Kepler and Leibnitz! Yet our academia only eulogizes NEWTON.

While, SHAKESPEARE'S plays are truly wonderful, it is beyond circumstantial evidence that the actor SHAKESPEARE was an illiterate person incapable of producing these works. It is very likely that these were the collective works of a "committee," writing under the "nominee" called SHAKESPEARE for the glory of England.

The up shoot is quite simple. Now that we are a superpower, we must promote our own heroes and not hang on to the coattails of our former colonial masters. Hanging on to GREAT BRITAIN'S coattails has brought us only grief and embarrassment.

Here are some of the entanglements we have been in where we were lured in by our former colonial masters:

1) The Hessian propaganda... (that's why we still put Germans into the category of second class citizens).

2) The Newton propaganda... (that's why we still don't have a solution to the multi body gravitational problem {larger than 2}).

3) Vietnam.... both France and Great Britain lured us into this morass by their DOMINO THEORY and made us renege the promise we made to HO CHI MIN to grant him independence

as soon as WW II would end. He fought Japan and Vichy France singlehandedly, without ANY AID FROM ANYONE!

4) Somalia.... we never had any interest in that area, but Great Britain, France and Italy did...

5) YUGOSLAVIA...who's interests are we fighting for? As far as history is concerned, Croatia, Slovenia and Bosnia Herzogovina are "provinces" which once belonged to the old HOLY ROMAN EMPIRE and now that the new Holy Roman Empire is emerging again we were conned, to wrestle these lands from Yugoslavia. Wars are very expensive, so, let Bubus Americanus do it.

6) KUWAIT......who's interests are we fighting for? As far as history is concerned KUWAIT was a province of IRAQ. After World War I, when the OTTOMAN EMPIRE was dismembered, this territory was carved out for the British supporters, provided the British would manage the portfolio for them.

So, a humanitarian case was fabricated and we stormed in as liberators.

7) AXIS OF EVIL...are we ready to fight the ARAB WORLD? Will we be testing the ARAB will and solidarity, if there is any? The danger is that this could become the largest and most devastating conflict human civilization has ever seen. (Iraq, Iran, Korea).

8) TRIAL OF MILOSOVICH...in Nürnberg we tried a few German hoodlums for their atrocities during World War II. Now that Germany will lead Europe again, this stain needs to be white washed. So, we pick a minor hoodlum and make a grand spectacle of it. Thus, Nürnberg will be cleansed... As per Wagner's Götterdämmerung...

9) AFGHANISTAN...Ostensibly we went into Afghanistan to punish the Taliban and avenge 9/11. But, the Taliban had nothing to do with 9/11, most of the terrorists were SAUDIS.

The Soviet Union spent 10 years in Afghanistan and they could not conquer them. What makes us think that we would do any better? Again we were drawn into a senseless war by a few war industrialists. They made all the profit and the little people of America paid the price!

10) IRAQ...We used to have a staunch opponent to IRAN in Iraq. Now we eliminated him. Isn't it like shooting yourself in the foot? We destroyed our best ally in that region!
Meanwhile Iraq is turning out worse than Afghanistan. Why don't we get out and stay out. But, Iraq is a British client so let Bubus Americanus restore Iraq to English control again.

Now, let me ask you, are our actions those of a "grown up" mature nation or the actions of BUBUS AMERICANUS, as the British call us?

Final test...generally speaking, this group is relatively well educated. Let me ask you this: WHICH AMERICAN INVENTOR/S invented the two forms of ELECTRICITY: AC...DC? And which is more important in our daily lives??? (Take a poll... Cite World's fair in St. Louis at the turn of the 19th century...Anglo Saxon mystique...).

George J. Kandiew

When my father was murdered by the Soviets, Emilia became a widow at 29 with two small children on her hands. Generally speaking, the Bolsheviks left no loose ends, so she knew from that day on, her goose was cooked if she ever lived in a SOVIET occupied state. Some charge would be drummed up and she would be sent at best, for an extended Siberian vacation. Then, her children would be orphans, and she could not bear that thought. So, she began racking her brain on how to escape the long arm of the Bolsheviks. Her solution was AMERICA, but how to get there was an entirely different problem. (It should be noted that Ukrainian literature laments often: "When will we have our George Washington?") Once, she came to this realization, she accepted the job as Assistant to the Mayor in the KURINIV district in Kiyiv.

At 29, Emilia was not only good looking, but a stunning woman. She was slender, dressed very nicely but always on the conservative side. She never wore lipstick or rouge, yet her lips were always naturally red and her cheeks blushed with natural color. Occasionally she would use a touch of plain powder to cover her "shiners." Her motto was: "Give us powder and perfume to perplex the dummies," which is loosely translated and does not rhyme too well in English. But, it not only rhymes well in Ukrainian and Russian but has a special "zing" to it, which accentuates superficiality.

She had long brown hair which she wore in braids. But, her most attractive feature was her pensive smile and her blue piercing eyes. She was composure in personification. Practically nothing could derail her composure especially in critical moments. Once the calamity was over, she might cry her heart out. But then, she would regain her composure and turn into a will of steel. Her signature was meticulous. She did not sign it, she painted it. She was often complimented on her beautiful signature, and in later years I would only mumble: "So had Robespierre." In short she had a will of steel, she was exceptionally talented in practically every discipline she took a fancy in, and was compassionate to a point of self destruction. This was her way to live life to its fullest.

The German war machine practiced TOTAL WAR. That is, it included a department which was specifically geared to promote "ANTI BOLSHEVIK" propaganda. For that, they needed willing collaborators who were fluent in RUSSIAN, were devout "Anti Bolsheviks" and would do their work for them eagerly. George fit that bill to a tee and worked in that department. At first he was an editor and then he was promoted to chief editor. He was a former student of the St. Petersburg school of Journalism and his command of the Russian language was superb. He had the knack of choosing not only the right words but words with the correct innuendo for the occasion.

He escaped St. Petersburg after the Bolsheviks murdered his stepfather and he never forgave them for that. He lived with his mother ANNA and his daughter MARIA in Kiyiv (Kiev when russified) when the Germans occupied the city.

Anna (his mother), had an affair with Plehve junior, who's father was the Minister of Interior in the Czarist regime. Plehve senior, among other things, was the architect of the CZARIST pogroms. He orchestrated them carefully and diligently, to occur only in the UKRAINE, so that world opinion would be directed in outrage at the Ukraine and not at "Mother Russia."

When Anna realized she was pregnant, she confronted her lover, but he would have no part of her. Undaunted, she made an appointment with Plehve senior, stating that she had a "grave personal matter to discuss" and was given an audience. She then presented her case, stressing that she was destitute.

Plehve listened attentively, took her address and told her he would get back to her but then, he added, "never to show her face in his office again."

Within a week or so, a messenger arrived. He offered her some money to tie her over and presented a plan. He was a bachelor, named JAKOV KANDIEW, who was a bit older than her, and was looking for a wife. Arrangements were made so that she could marry him and live in relative comfort. Should she not accept this offer, she need not bother "his greatness ever again." So, Anna accepted the offer, got married to Jakov, and as it turned out, he was a very decent man.

His origin is somewhat vague, but it seems he was of Turkic extraction from the island of CRETE. George was born in 1902 and Plehve senior was "executed" by Bolshevik agitators in 1904.

George finished high school at 17 and entered the SCHOOL of JOURNALISM in St. Petersburg. He rented a room in a 3 room flat, right in the center of town. Jakov paid all expenses while George corresponded with him and his mother. George spoke always fondly of Jakov each time the topic came up.

By 1923, St. Petersburg was in a state of chaos. Money meant nearly nothing since Lenin was spending his German Marks furiously to promote the revolution and Trotzky tried to match him at every turn with the AMERICAN dollars he kept receiving from NEW YORK CITY, from a committee to promote the revolution in Russia, as flaunted in "OUR CROWD." So, Trotzky was funded by "the Who's Who of the American Jewry," while Lenin tried to spent a railroad car loaded with GERMAN Marks to break the backbone of the Czarist regime.

According to George, money meant nothing then, since so much of it was circulating fast and furious in these chaotic days in St. Petersburg. George used the analogy of a gambling casino. After you have played fast and furiously all night, with fortunes changing hands with each roll of the dice, the value of money is lost and has no meaning.

However, in that fatal year Jakov was murdered by Bolsheviks and George's honeymoon in St. Petersburg seemed to be over. But then, in the midst of this chaos a new opportunity arose.

All landlords were "expropriated." That is, they lost their personal property and their property became communal property overnight. At the same time the currency was reset to denomination in gold.

It so happened that George's landlord had gone to the Crimea to recuperate, leaving George with the only keys to the flat. And, while officially all property became communal, a flat in St. Petersburg, in the center of town, was worth a fortune on the black market. Anyone who had political aspirations in the new regime was willing to pay a small fortune for such a flat. So, George found a buyer, and sold the "keys" for 20,000 gold rubles, which was a small fortune in those days. George moved out of the flat and moved into the best hotel in town.

In no time at all he had a small entourage of friends. George fell in love with Natalie, who was of Polish extraction. They got married in a truly modern fashion (they registered their marriage in the new Department for Family Affairs). Natalie got pregnant, and MARIA was born in 1938. But, by 1940 the money ran out. And, when Natalie found out that they had spent his fortune, she left him and her infant. So, a heartbroken and destitute George, took Maria to his mother and together they moved to KIYIV to seek a new opportunity.

While in St. Petersburg, George witnessed another "Russian Institution" which had an everlasting effect on him. These were the "DEBTORS PITS." They were usually located at the edge of the local market, since the market was the blood line for survival in Russia. Practically every market in Czarist Russia had them. They were holes, about a yard square on the top, and about 12 feet deep. The top had a iron mesh cover which could be locked. They were used to "imprison" debtors. That is, when someone borrowed money and did not repay his debt in the allotted time, that debtor was literally thrown into such a hole until he rotted to death or repaid his debt. Consequently, once a debtor experienced this ordeal, he was willing to sell his soul to be relieved of the punishment, and usually they would sell their daughters into prostitution to settle their debt when all other assets were depleted.

The bottom was usually wet and infested with rats, because helpful samaritans would throw food into these pits, and if the poor creature did not catch it, it landed on the bottom of the pit and attracted all sorts of animals. By the end of one day in such a pit, good part of the feet were gnawed away by the beasts and within a week the poor creature was as good as dead even if fed properly by his relatives.

George witnessed many destitute creatures in such pits and consequently HE NEVER BORROWED MONEY from anybody. In fact, he never had a checking account in his life; for he believed that this was a capitalist tool to ensnare gullible debtors. Even when he lived in NEW YORK CITY he had no checking account and paid his bills either in person or with Money Orders!

The debtors pits were introduced first in the UKRAINE, when the Polish Barons were invited by the Lithuanians to rule parts of the Ukraine which the LITHUANIANS occupied after the Tartar invasion, during the Jagellon dynasty starting in the 15th century. With the Polish Barons came the Jewish moneylenders, since Christians were not allowed to lend money and charge interest at that time.

The cost of money was often between 70 to 100 percent a year. Thus, many uninformed farmers became quickly and irrevocably indebted and enslaved. The Duchy of Muscovy thought of the debt holes so highly that they became a standard fixture throughout their Duchy. And, with Peter the Great they became standard features throughout Czarist Russia. They were used in the collection of financial or tax debts.

The most prominent person arising from the debt pits, was Czarina Catherine I, the second wife of Czar Peter the Great. Catherine's father was a small Lithuanian landowner who borrowed money and was unable to repay it. He was thrown into a debt pit. Her father sold Catherine into prostitution to get his release. She was bought by Menshikov, a friend of Czar Peter. Since Czar Peter had sent his first wife into a nunnery because of her sexual inadequacy, he was in need for a woman. When Menshikov noticed that Czar Peter liked Catherine, he gifted her to him. For most of the years together she was his sex slave. But, when Czar Peter was captured by the Ottoman Sultan in the Pruth campaign (1710), and Catherine ransomed him with her own jewels, a grateful Czar Peter married her when they returned to St. Petersburg.

In any event, Emilia and George met and became friends. From then on, starting in May 1942, George would come and visit us at our home. As far as I could tell, he was a city person. He was not interested in gardening or our farm animals. But, he was very articulate and well informed about the war and the Soviet political infrastructure. This was also the time when the war was taking on a bad turn for the Germans.

Vlasov was given a free hand by Stalin and organized a successful campaign against the Finns and Norwegians in the North and then, in the dead of winter of 1941, he launched a massive counterattack along the entire front of about 1000 miles against the Germans and their allies, and for the first time the Germans were in retreat. Many of his soldiers were political prisoners who Stalin released for his army, and allowed them "to earn their freedom."

Visions of a Napoleonic rout were on everyone's mind. But, Hitler broadcast every day, demanding that the Wehrmacht not retreat an inch. Still, Vlasov pushed back the German front about 125 miles, and in some areas as much as 300 miles. But then, the unthinkable happened. Vlasov changed sides and surrendered to the Germans in the spring of 1942.

Apparently what happened was Vlasov's success changed Stalin's mind. And, when Vlasov's champaign ran out of steam, Stalin ordered the political prisoners to be arrested again, which Vlasov had integrated into his army, and to whom he personally had promised a pardon if they fought well. He established his headquarters at Volkhov, near St. Petersburg which was still under siege. But, when the KGB came for him, he knew his goose was cooked. So, Vlasov, his staff and his soldiers defected to the Germans. Vlasov offered to fight for the Germans and claimed that he could rally as many as 35 million soldiers to fight Stalin. This became known as the VLASOV MOVEMENT. But, German Hubris would not let that happen.

Hitler was determined to win the war all by himself and his present allies. So, Vlasov and all his soldiers were imprisoned by the Germans! And, they stayed in German prison until mid 1944, when the war was practically lost. Only then was Vlasov and his soldiers allowed to fight on the German side, in German uniform. When the war ended,

Vlasov became a political hot potato. He tried to surrender to general Patton but, general Eisenhower would not allow Patton to accept his surrender. Instead, a British colonel was allowed to accept Vlasov's surrender. He promptly turned Vlasov and his soldiers over to the Soviets. Now, the KGB moved in. They whisked Vlasov and his Adjutant on a special train to Moscow where they were both hung with piano wire in Moscow's RED SQUARE. Vlasov's officers were lined up and shot. And, his soldiers were herded into cattle cars and sent for a SIBERIAN VACATION; 20 years of hard labor and the loss of human rights. And, of course, Vlasov's credits were ERASED, just like the Egyptians used to do on their monuments.

Instead Vlasov's credits were heaped on the new darling of Stalin, Marshall ZHUKOV. At the end of the war, Patton tried to return hastily to the US, probably to expose this fiasco to President Truman. But, a "stray bullet," killed that gallant soldier. To this day, the US involvement in that plot is still a government secret...

Thus, Vlasov amputated the German ARMY GROUP NORTH at Moscow and by the end of 1942, ZHUKOV amputated ARMY GROUP SOUTH at STALINGRAD. And, by the summer of 1943 the Germans and Soviets faced each other in the greatest and most decisive land battle ever fought at KURSK (July 1943), and the Germans lost. Thus, the German ARMY GROUP CENTER was amputated by ZHUKOV and now the Germans were in full retreat along the entire front.

(It should be noted that before the Battle of Kursk, Hitler sued for peace with Stalin. Molotov and von Ribbentropp met and tried to negotiate a peace. Stalin wanted the "OLD POLISH BORDER," while Hitler wanted a new border where Ukraine, Belarus and the Baltic states were part of the "NEW GROSSLAND." That is, part of the new WESTERN EUROPE. Much of the trouble in the Ukraine today stems from this "Hitler's Europe," which goes under the new name of "European Union," as it encroaches on Russia).

Once the Soviets won at KURSK, our days in the Soviet Union were numbered. Emilia got permission to take the last train from KIYIV to BERLIN. And, with us was GEORGE with his family, his daughter

Masha and his mother Anna. When we left KIYIV in October 1943, we could hear faintly the heavy guns of the Soviets bombarding the German positions...

Our train was attacked by partisans near Proskurov. While we retreated to town, I got sick and had to be hospitalized for a short time. During that time Emilia found a cushy job. The commandant of that area accidentally shot himself in his hand. So when Emilia applied for a job he hired her immediately because she had a medical degree. She cleaned his wound and he was on his way to recovery. When he started paying too much attention to her, Emilia married George, who adopted Emma and me. As soon as I was released from the hospital we continued our journey to Berlin.

While in Berlin, George suffered a concussion when our bunker suffered a direct hit, everybody else was ok. The concussion turned out to be a blessing for George, because he was therewith exempt from all manual labor. In particular right after the war when every able bodied person was used to clean up the "battlefields of Berlin."

Emilia was not that lucky. She was drafted into a pool of four women (all with medical experience) who were dressed up into rubber outfits, in addition they were handed rubber boots, gloves, goggles, a rubber cap and a huge meat hook to drag out the dead bodies out of tanks and other vehicles and load them into mortuary trucks. For months Emilia had the most terrifying nightmares.

When the Soviets stabilized Berlin, they opened a Russian library and a Russian Orthodox Church. In his naivete, George went to the library and signed up (with a false name and false address). The first few visits were uneventful. But on the third visit, he was arrested. Eventually, we got word "through the grapevine" that he was "repatriated to Mother Russia."

At that point his mother Anna, took Masha and repatriated voluntarily to the Soviet Union, in the hope of finding her son. All the pleading by Emilia to leave Masha with us was of no use.
One day she simply disappeared with Masha.

About two months later George showed up from out of the blue. He was deported alright, but he had escaped and worked his way back to Berlin and our residence.

Then, in early 1949, Emilia got caught by SMERSH, an arm of the KGB. Emilia was beaten but released, because one of our neighbors was Dr. Derz, a high ranking member of the SED, a left wing party in Berlin.

When Emilia arrived, both Emilia and George went to the commandant of the British sector, we lived in the British sector and asked for political asylum, which they received. Within a few days we left Berlin. But, George, Kathy and I ended up in Cornberg, while Emilia and Emma ended up in Wiesbaden, after Eleanor Roosevelt intervened, because Emma was very sick and needed space in a "hospital plane."

It was customary at the time to be "DE NAZIFIED" by the allied intelligence, which was located in Mittenwald, Bavaria. So, we were shipped to Mittenwald and there George and Emilia underwent "DE NAZIFICATION" procedures. When they were cleared we were allowed to leave.

Emilia had secured a key to an apartment in Munich, right at the foot of the English Garden (a large park in Munich). Emilia worked as a nurse, Emma was attending Munich University, I was attending a Real Gymnasium, Kathy attended elementary school, while George "guarded" our apartment.

Eventually we got our own apartment on Wehrle Strasse near Herkomer Platz. George landed a job with RADIO LIBERTY as chief editor in the Russian section and Emma landed a job at Radio Liberty in the Ukrainian section. Emma became the primary newscaster in the Ukrainian section. Thus, when the Ukraine became independent in 1989, Emma became a household name in the Ukraine. In addition, Emma has published over 50 books so far, all in Ukrainian and she has become a modern art painter with three dedicated museums in the Ukraine exhibiting her art works. She has been nominated three times for a Nobel Prize in literature.

However, in 1957 the KGB nearly caught George again. This time in broad daylight in the center of town. A car pulled up, two men jumped out, grabbed George and tried to drag him into their car. George being tall and lanky fought them off as hard as he could, all the while screaming at the top of his lungs for help. Almost instantly bystanders came to his aid and tore him away from the clutches of the KGB. George was shaking like a leaf even when he came home and told Emilia. She calmed him down, took him by his arm and together they went to the American Embassy and applied to emigrate to the USA. They were accepted and a date was set for our departure.

George got a job transfer to New York since the main office of Radio Liberty was in Manhattan. George lasted exactly one month. George acted like a "prima donna" and that was just not tolerated. Thus, from then on he worked for the HOBOE NEWS (as it is called by all Ukrainians). In Russian it is pronounced: novoje russkoje slovo, meaning NEW RUSSIAN WORD. Since his salary hardly paid the rent, Emilia had to start working again. This time she worked as a private duty nurse. A placement agency found her a family of five, ages 93 to 72. The youngest was William, all others were women.

In 1976 William (the last member) died and included Emilia in his will. She got the apartment on Riverside Drive and 78th Street, the contents of the apartment and a trust fund. The fund was structured in such a way that she could withdraw the interest and $5,000 annually. But, as interest rates were rising her bond fund was declining in value. (I tried to explain to her what was happening, but she just could not understand it).

When George saw this new wealth, he decided to start a love affair with a girl of 19 something, called Lila, a friend of Cathy. Emilia wanted a divorce but George refused. So, Emilia got it anyway in Florida. Then, Emilia divided the cash and the contents of the apartment and they parted company. (George refused to have any part of the properties since they had mortgages). The "CHIPPY" loved him for his poetry, while George was 74. When George's money ran out the chippy left him for another "artsy" oldtimer. George got himself an elderly lady friend, called Alla.

By then Emilia lived in Warm Mineral Springs, Florida. One day she received a phone call from George who called to tell Emilia that he was coming down to Florida. To which Emilia replied, "...if you do, the local cops will be waiting for you."

George died in 1984 and was buried by Alla.

Meanwhile, Masha used the RED CROSS to locate her father. Around 1965 she located George and began correspondence. As it turned out she and her grandmother Anna Simonina went first to St. Petersburg (Leningrad). When they could not find George there they moved to Kiyiv and stayed with Emilia's mother, also named Anna. At some point the two Anna's had a mayor quarrel and Anna Simonina left with Masha. Shortly thereafter Anna Simonina died and Masha was put into an orphanage.

In the orphanage Masha learned typing skills and decided to locate her natural mother. She found her mother living in the Crimea, married to an official of the KGB. He got Masha a job as a typist.

When George received the first few letters he had no idea what to do. At first he was afraid to respond. But, then he checked with the authorities and they encouraged him to respond.

Thus began their correspondence.

According to Emilia, Masha kept inquiring about me. George kept telling her that I was in the "MOVING BUSINESS" and that he had no address for me. Neither George nor Emilia would tell me about Masha until they got divorced. At the same time Masha asked for "merchandise" she could use in the Soviet Black Market: Blue Jeans, coats, dresses and other items. While George and Emilia were still together Emilia felt very sorry for Masha and bought her new merchandise she asked for from Macy's and Bloomingdale's. But, after the divorce Emilia felt she was out of the picture. Thus, when George was with Lila all "care packages" stopped. And, when George was with Alla, they would send Masha used stuff. Then George died in 1984 and all care packages to Masha stopped altogether. However Masha continued her correspondence with Alla.

In time Masha got a "Student Visa" and stayed with Alla in New York City. Alla got her a job in the "health care" industry.

While Masha stayed with Alla they decided to co mingle their savings account. Thus, when one winter Alla fell in front of a restaurant, she broke her hip and collected $50,000, which Alla deposited into their joint savings account. Shortly thereafter Alla died and Masha "inherited" the savings account. Next Masha got her boyfriend to New York. He found a job as a taylor.

Shortly thereafter Masha located Cathy in Connecticut. But after a few visits Cathy told Masha off and broke up with her. By 1994 Marinella, my second wife, and I divorced. I decided to take care of my mother. So, I joined her in Warm Mineral Springs. We had a marvelous time even though Emilia was in a wheelchair. We were going to the beach, to the Malls in Sarasota, Venice and North Fort Mayers, and at night we would watch opera, musicals and movies. During the day Emilia maintained the best garden in Warm Mineral Springs. We grew oranges, grapefruits (pink and white), bananas, papayas, bay leafs, "Japanese Plums," and one patch of the most gorgeous lilies (see picture on the back cover).

Well, one day we got a call from Masha. I spoke to her and I was genuinely moved when I heard her. She called back a few times and we arranged for her to visit us. She came with her boyfriend (Boris) and I picked them up at the Sarasota Airport. Next time Masha came with her granddaughter, Julia. This time things did not go too well. Julia wanted to go to the beach, while Masha wanted to go to "our" lake in Warm Mineral Springs. So, I took Julia to the Venice beach while Masha stayed with Emilia. When I came home I landed in a field of "firecrackers." Everybody was excited and upset. Masha was ready to take the next plane back to New York, which was possible only the next morning. So, the next morning I took Masha and Julia to the airport and that is the last I have seen of her.

So, what happened? Emilia told me the following story. It seems that Masha had planned this encounter with Emilia from the beginning. As soon as I had left with Julia to go to the beach, Emilia and Masha had a long conversation about what happened in the past. Then, Masha started to project her future. How she needed to find someone her age with assets, with a pension and some cash. Since she and I were not directly related she wanted to marry me. At that point Emilia blew her stack, told her to get out, and never to come back.

Thus, our beautiful friendship ended for good.

From Kiyiv to Berlin

After the Battle of Kursk in July 1943, our stay in Kiyiv (Kiev when russified) was at an end. My father had been murdered on the order of Khrushchev, and we were next, if caught by the Soviets. My mother Emilia had secured a "Marschbefehl" to Berlin. According to Emilia, we left on the last train to Berlin. Our family was: Emilia, my mother; Emma, my sister and I. Emma was 7 years older than I. Travelling with us was George and his family. His mother Anna and his daughter Masha. Masha was about my age.

Our train was ambushed by partisans near Proskurov. I got sick and needed to be hospitalized. During that time, Emilia married George. George adopted Emma and me, and we resumed our journey to Berlin.

Finally, we were on our way again. I remember sitting on the window side. I was glued to the window to see something, but we still travelled by night and the only thing I saw, if I strained very hard, was silhouettes in the moonlight. I must have been glued for hours to the window this way, but there was really not much to see, so I cuddled up to my mother and fell asleep. Surely we had left the UKRAINE by now...

***

How did the word UKRAINE originate? How did the colors in her flag originate? And, how did the strange TRIPOD originate? Archaeologically speaking, Kiyiv was an ancient city dating back more than 2,500 years. Many argue that it could be much older than that when you consider the TRYPILLIAN excavations. Artifacts there have been carbon dated to 4500 BC and older!!

Kiyiv existed already when HERODOTUS lived in OLBIA about 500 BC. Herodotus lived there 8 years; he even married a native girl who bore him 3 children. But, then his "Wanderlust" took hold of him and he left her and his children, she was only a "barbarian" to him.

In his histories he dedicated an entire chapter to her: MELPAMENE. The Greeks called the residents of Ukraine SCYTHIANS. But, according to STRABO the word SCYTHIANS was a generic name. It meant the people living to the north of Greece in the cold climate, just like the word ETHIOPIANS, meant the people living to the south of EGYPT, in the hot climate.

The story is about DARIUS the Great and how he and his great army were nearly annihilated in the UKRAINE. In early Greek history, the initial sagas all occurred on the shores of the BLACK SEA: JASON and the Argonauts occurred before the TROJAN war. How do we know? Well, Achilles and Ulysses were only boys at that time and Hercules was still alive and a member of their party. By the time of the TROJAN war, Hercules was already dead.

The southern shore of the Ukraine and the Crimea were Greek colonies. These colonies were as much needed by Greece as by the Scythians. Along that shore were major trading centers. And, according to Strabo more than 6 million bushels of wheat and other grains changed hands between the Ukrainians and the Greeks.

During the PELEPONESE war, Athens lost her major colonies and access to the other "grain centers" of the known world after their debacle at SYRACUSE in 417 BC. Access to NORTH AFRICA and EGYPT was lost shortly thereafter. Yet, the Athenians could not be starved into submission until 401; not until the SPARTANS, with the aid of the PERSIANS, blockaded the SEA of MARMARA, and thus cut off the trade with the UKRAINE.

The GOTHIC empire stretched from the river ELBE to the URAL mountains, and from the BALTIC SEA to the river DANUBE, and the BLACK SEA. Then, the Black Sea was called the Euxine Sea and the Azov Sea was called the LAKE of MOESIA.

The Goths organized into kingdoms. Often each had their own name. In antiquity, before the Trojan war, the Goths and Slavs merged into one people by exchanging their kings. Their name could be Slavic or Gothic which was expressed in their name as a suffix. When it ended in ryc or ric it was Gothic and when it ended in slav or mir it was slavic. Western historians often modified the ending. Thus, the ending slav was often spelled as laus and so on.

The Macedonians originated at the lake of MOESIA, which makes them the original ancestors of the DON area, which was part of the UKRAINE. Sometimes after the TROJAN war, the Macedonians began their move for a better homeland. They crossed over to the Danube, and after the PERSIAN war, they invaded the Balkans. Then, with Philip and Alexander they conquered the Greeks. And, ultimately, Alexander conquered the PERSIAN EMPIRE with his MACEDONIAN GOTHS, the Greeks were only a small contingent in his force. They were the GREEK MERCENARIES. All of Alexander's generals and leaders were GOTHS. And, when ALEXANDER died, his empire was divided among his loyal GOTHIC generals: Ptolemy got EGYPT; Seluchius got PERSIA and Antiochus got GREECE and SYRIA.

Even ARISTOTLE was not a Greek, he came from MILETUS and taught in ATHENS, and when the word got out that he may suffer the same fate as SOCRATES, his master, he left for MILETUS.

According to TACITUS, the only Gothic people, the SUEVE went beyond the river Elbe and settled near the Rhine in central Germany. The original German land was bound by the rivers RHINE, ELBE and DANUBE. Once Germany was created in 1870, in Versailles, the Sueve were declared to be GERMAN, they called them "Schwaben."

In fact many historical events were settled by "DECLARATION" by the Germans. For example: The King in Prussia; the location where the Roman general Varus in 9 AD was ambushed and defeated in "Germany." In 1905 a commission was created to find that location. They did, by declaration, without a shred of historical evidence. Varus was defeated by Arminius (which is a Gothic name) yet the monument erected was to "Herman the German."

About 50 BC, a Gothic expedition moved into today's DENMARK, SWEDEN and NORWAY with ODIN, loosely translated in UKRAINIAN "The Only One." Along the river Elbe settled the GOTHIC JüTES, SASSONS (whom the Germans forged to be SAXONS) and the WENDS. The Sassons and Wends were exterminated by the GERMANS during the era of the Crusades and a new "MARK" was formed. This became the origin of Brandenburg and only in the 13th century, with the invasion of the TARTARS, was BERLIN founded. Then, to add insult to injury, the GOTHIC PRUSSIANS were conquered, exterminated and the GERMANS took their name to boot. Thus, PRUSSIA was formed. This became the "landed" German nobility called "JUNKERS" with a title of "von."

During the time of AUGUSTUS CAESAR, when the GREAT ROMAN CENSUS was taken, the ROMANS with all their dominions numbered about 5.2 million inhabitants, with about 260,000 legionnaires spread throughout the Empire. At that time, the GOTHS took also a census and they numbered about 5.9 million. Thus, the Gothic Empire was slightly larger than the Roman Empire at its peak.

Western historians, distinguish between the Visigoths or western Goths and Ostrogoths or eastern GOTHS. This distinction was made when the Goths accepted CHRISTIANITY, albeit the ARIAN form. The VISIGOTHS were Christians, while the OSTROGOTHS were still heathens when the HUNS invaded their Empire. Eventually, many OSTROGOTHS became Arian Christians also. Once the HUNS were destroyed, the modern era of the UKRAINE started. The Russians called the OSTROGOTHS: RUS. However, the only valid usage of RUS is Kiyivan Ryc (Rus), meaning Kiyivan Kings. Hence RUS equals KING. Roughly half of the Goths left their homeland in terror from the Huns. The eastern most Goths, the Alans left first. They settled eventually near Orleans. Then, the Visigoths left. Half of them moved to the Danube to seek sanctuary in the Christian Roman Empire, because they were Christians, Arian Christians.

But they did not know that the Roman Empire took on a new form of Christianity, Orthodoxy, about 10 years before the Goths appeared on the border running from the Huns (under Emperor Valens, and Arianism was declared a heresy).

The Goths asked for sanctuary and got it, but they had to turn over their weapons and give their children as hostages. They were promised fertile land to sustain themselves, but got arid land instead. Then, they got word that their children were slaughtered because they refused conversion to the Orthodox faith. So, they send a messenger back to their homeland asking to be rescued.

Back in their homeland the remaining Goths called for a SBOR (ALLTHING) in the Trypillian area and elected ALARIC as King to save the mistreated kinsmen. Alaric came, liberated the Goths and decided to move them out of the Balkans.

In Constantinople ruled the "Augustus Caesar" while in Rome ruled a "Caesar," an underling of Augustus Caesar, Honorius.

His general was Stilicho. Honorius ordered Stilicho to destroy the Goths as they crossed over from the Balkans into Italy. But, Stilicho was a Goth, who refused to attack the Gothic migration. Therefore, Honorius recalled Stilicho to Rome and had him murdered at a banquet. Alaric found out and decided to punish Honorius.

Alaric planned to take Rome. But when he arrived and looked at Rome's fortifications he knew he could not take Rome by force. So, he resorted to a ruse. He handpicked 300 young men. They were given instructions to overwhelm the guards at the next full moon at a specific gate, as soon as it got dark. Then, Alaric left a messenger for the Romans and left with his entire army. The message was that Alaric left these young men for Rome as slaves. So, when the Romans came out and saw these young men and got the message, they took them in readily.

Alaric returned at the next full moon, the designated gate was opened and Alaric sacked Rome in 410 AD. After 3 days of plunder the Goths left and continued their way to southern Italy where they planned to take passage to North Africa where the Alans and Vandals had established a Kingdom under Genseric near "old Carthage."

However, Alaric died and was buried in the Busento River. Then, the Goths decided to take the "land route" to Africa. So, they turned around and trekked north. When they came to Rome again, they sacked it again in 411 AD, since some of the young men were still in Rome, they opened the gate for them.

This time the sack lasted 10 days. Thereafter, they trekked into Gaul where many rejoined the other Visigoths who had settled near BORDAUX. Later, the Visigoths were invited by the Roman Emperor to rule in Spain. And, if you look closely, you will find many Ukrainian names still in use today, in Spain and Latin America. For example: Perez, means pepper in Ukrainian; Galicia is a province in the Ukraine and in Spain. And so on...

By 451 AD, the leader of the Huns was Attila, while the Caesar in Rome was Valentinian III, who had a sister Honoria. Honoria had an affair with a Roman commoner and got pregnant. Valentinian promptly killed Honoria's lover. Now Honoria wanted revenge. She sent a letter (a proposal of marriage to Attila) telling him that her dowry was Gaul. Attila promptly accepted and demanded submission in Gaul. Valentinian rejected the "contract" and a war ensued between the Romans and the Huns. The problem was that Rome did not have a military to speak of. And, when Attila did not get satisfaction, he tried to enforce his contract with Honoria by force, by invading Gaul.

There was Aetius who commanded the Scythians (in the Ukraine). Therefore, the Alans from Orleans and the Visigoths from Bordeaux were recruited to defend whatever was still left of the Western Roman Empire. Thus, the forces of "Christendom" led by Theodoric the Visigoth King (all were Arian Christians) opposed the heathens led by Attila. They met at Chalons sur Marne (near Orlean in 451 AD). (The lineup was: On the Christian side: left wing the Visigoths, center the Alans, right wing the Scythians led by Aetius. On the heathen side: Right wing the Ostrogoths, center the Huns led by Attila, right wing the Alemani (Germans) and Burgundians). And, the Christians defeated the Huns. (This is how the derogatory name for the Germans originated as the "Huns." Much later it was confirmed by Kaiser Wilhelm when he told the Germans to fight like the "Huns").

The Christian forces defeated the Huns. But, since Theodoric was killed, western historians gave the leadership to Aetius. Verdi has even a great opera depicting part of that story, but Verdi rewrites history in a small way.

The upshot was that Goths dominated the growth and rulership in Gaul with the "Merowingian dynasty." Notice, the first king "Mir o veche" was not a RYC or RIC. He was a commoner, but the founder of the dynasty. However, his son was Chilperic I, with a long list of Chilperic's to follow. Eventually, the mayordomo took over the rule, the Carolingians with the help of the Patriarch of Rome.

Chilperic I is a very interesting case, because he killed his wife and had to flee to Thuringia. There he was contacted by legates from Rome and changed his faith to the Roman faith. Then, he returned to the land of his father and converted the Merowingians to the Roman faith. This gave him status and prestige and many historians called him by his new name: Clovis.

Clovis made war on the Alans (Orleans) and Visigoths (Bordeaux) and conquered them. Then, the Carolingians moved in and took over the leadership from them with Karl Martell. Followed by the Pippin's and then Charlemagne, which is a Latin name, not a French one. Collectively they are called Franks.

The Patriarch of Rome wanted to be leader of the Christian Church. But, there was still a powerful Roman Empire in Constantinople. Therefore, in order to call himself Pope and leader of Christendom, the Pope needed a powerful protector. Thus, the Patriarch of Rome made a concordat with Charlemagne. The Patriarch promoted himself to Pope and leader of Christendom and crowned Charlemagne as Emperor of the Holy Roman Empire. This pact was to be valid in perpetuity, that is forever. All the titles of the Roman Emperor were bestowed on the Holy Roman Emperor, including the title of Pontifex Maximus, which later caused the battle for the "INVESTITURE," when the Pope demanded that title back. Of course, in the end the Pope won.

At that time the Goths dominated Gaul. Thus, to prevent a takeover by the Goths an "ELECTORATE" was created, which elected the Holy

Roman Emperors. Initially it consisted of 4 bishops and 3 dukes. After the Pope won the battle for the investiture, the electorate was changed to 4 bishops and 5 dukes.

The word RUS originated from a Chronicle of Kiyiv which was found in the 15th century and which was hailed as an original. In any event, the RUS had a powerful state, which was divided into many PRINCIPALITIES: Kiyiv, Novgorod, Tver, Pskov, Lviv and so on. Their King ruled from KIYIV, while his designated successor ruled from NOVGOROD. (This is where the designation of "Prince of Wales" originates in England, since it was ruled by Goths from 1066 to 1377).

That is, there was a PECKING ORDER among the Princes. As they got closer to inherit the rule, they were moved to the next higher ranking principality. We know this was so, because in one episode in the Chronicle, the CITY ELDERS came to KIYIV and presented their grievance to the KING'S COURT: They said in effect: "Let us have a more permanent PRINCE because each time we 'fatten him up,' he is moved to another PRINCIPALITY..."

The RUS founded many cities, over 200, but, MOSCOW was not one of them. Most cities were FOUNDED and CHARTERED. That is, the residents had many DEMOCRATIC privileges. They had recourse in their principality, first with the PRINCELY COURT; then, they had recourse RINGING THE LIBERTY BELL and be judged by their peers, called VECHE or THING; then they had recourse in the KING'S COURT in KIYIV and if that failed they could present their claim in a SBOR or ALLTHING, represented by all Principalities.

The reason for this structure was that FREEDOM and JUSTICE were the dominant themes. The Rus had no SERFS or SLAVES, these institutions were introduced by the TARTARS, MUSCOVY and POLAND. And, the RUS did not practice OSTRACISM.

Because, there were so many Princes, some Principalities were "dead ends," within the hierarchy to the throne. We are so fond of the Greek Democracy, yet practically every GREAT GREEK leader was Ostracized and lived out his old age with his arch enemies. For example:

Themistocles, the Greek hero of SALAMIS, who defeated the PERSIAN fleet, was ostracized and lived out his old age in the PERSIAN EMPIRE, supported by the PERSIAN ruler! So did ALCIPIADES, and so on, the list could be made endless.

Thus, the PRINCIPALITY of KIYIV, included the cities: CHERNIHIV, PEREYASLAVL, LVIV and many others. However, this PRINCIPALITY the scribe IPATIV, at the time of King YAROSLAV the WISE in the 11th century, called the UKRAINE. Their flag was BLUE and YELLOW, the same colors as SWEDEN and the distinctive TRIPOD was a symbol of PERUN or POSEIDON and symbolized the THREE branches of the GOTHS. That is: VISIGOTHS, OSTROGOTHS and ALANS.

Their land stretched from BRATISLAVA in SLOVAKIA (founded and chartered by King Sviatoslav from Kiyiv), to MOLDAVIA, GALICIA, PODOLIA, the present day UKRAINE, the DON and the KUBAN. It was the largest principality in Kiyivan RYC (RUS), followed by NOVHOROD and BELARUS in size. From 800 to 1240, the Ukraine was the largest and most powerful country in Europe.

The Byzantine Empire could only be strong and well provided for as long as the Ukraine was strong. When the Ukraine was destroyed by the Tartars the Byzantine Empire was destroyed also, because the Ukraine provided the muscle (legionnaires) and the food (grains).

Alexander Nevsky was a Prince in Novhorod. One day a Swedish missionary showed up, Yarl Birger, and preached the Catholic faith. The city elders called Alexander Nevsky and told him to take his companions and "chase away" that missionary and his knights. Alexander took his companions, chased Yarl Birger into the swamps and butchered them all. The city elders were very upset and put him on notice that any further violation would cause his banishment.

At that time, the Tartars led by BATU, the grandson of Ghengis Khan was on the march to conquer Europe. Alexander Nevsky called the city elders and told them to ally themselves with Batu. The city elders were so upset that they banished Alexander. Thus, Alexander Nevsky became a Prince without a principality.

However, there was Moscow, a "watering hole" for robbers and outcasts. Alexander Nevsky turned to them and they welcomed him.

When the Tartars crossed into Europe, Alexander Nevsky went to Batu and offered him his services. He showed Batu which cities were important for the destruction of RUS. Thus, in 1240 the Tartars took Kiyiv, utterly destroyed the city, killed off most of the inhabitants and the rest were taken as slaves. Marco Polo travelled to China and on his way passed through Kiyiv and described the total destruction.

As it turned out, while Batu's main force laid siege to Andrianopolis, a messenger arrived requesting Batu to return to the capital because the great Khan Ugudai had been poisoned by a jealous concubine and a new Great Khan had to be elected. Thus, Batu turned his army around, took them east of Moscow to a place called Sarai. Then Batu went to the election. (His forward forces had reached the Elbe River. Thus, had it not been for the jealous concubine, Batu would have conquered all of Europe).

When Batu returned from the election he decided not to continue with his conquest but to live off the land he had conquered. The Tartars had learned, when they conquered China that the most efficient way to rule a conquered country was by installing the native princes. Thus, Batu organized an auction for the highest tribute to be paid to the Tartars. That is, each prince was allowed to bid for any principality he liked. Thus, the highest bidder received the principality. That became the tribute paid annually to Batu.

Of course, Alexander Nevsky received the principality of his choice at his price, for his valuable service to the Khan. Alexander chose VOLODIMIR (Vladimir when russified). There was only one problem, when Alexander moved to VOLODIMIR and started to rule "absolutely," he could not, because the city was founded and chartered. Eventually, Alexander gave up and moved to Moscow. Thus began the expansion of Muscovy!

Alexander Nevsky struck also a special deal with Batu. Alexander offered to collect all tributes and bring them to the Tartar Khan. This was acceptable to Batu and put Alexander Nevsky into a unique position where he controlled all the money. Thus, when a principality was not obedient to Alexander Nevsky, he would go to the Khan and complain that this principality rebelled and refused to pay their tribute. Then, the Tartars would go to that principality and punish them, usually by taking many to the slave markets.

In this way, slowly but surely one principality after another was taken over by Muscovy. Practically all other principalities were taken over by Muscovy by force and were integrated into MOTHER MUSCOVY, much later to become MOTHER RUSSIA.

This leaves us with the name of RUS. The Kiyivan Chronicle states in one episode, that the city elders formed a delegation with the following message: "Go to the land of RUS and tell them we have a rich land but we are leaderless, so come and rule over us..." The problem with the word RUS in Cyrillic is that it need not mean specifically RUS but RYC. How can this be? Remember, the UKRAINE was the melting pot of sorts, of GREEK and ROMAN cultures.

In antiquity, the GREEK colonies were practically sacred to the UKRAINIANS, all their trade was done in the CRIMEA and on the shore line of the Black Sea. The Greeks were replaced with ROMANS and while their alphabet was generally different, many letters were the same and depending on the mood of the reader, it was pronounced in Greek or Latin. For Example: The Latin name BARBARA was pronounced VARVARA. But then, conversion to Christianity came from CONSTANTINOPLE and there the OFFICIAL language was LATIN while the common language was GREEK.

Thus, when KING VOLODIMIR accepted Christianity, Kiyiv became a PATRIARCHATE, the only one in the entire land of RUS and Volodimir married the SISTER OF THE ROMAN EMPEROR (Basil II), the only such marriage in the ENTIRE HISTORY of THE ROMAN and BYZANTINE EMPIRE, a span of 2200 years! Most of the clergy came from CONSTANTINOPLE and they used GREEK and LATIN interchangeably.

Thus, the word RUS really meant RYC or RIC, that is a GOTHIC KING. What was so important about a GOTHIC KING that the KIYIVANS valued so much? The answer is: PERSONAL LIBERTIES. To the RUS, a KING was more of a JUDGE than ruler and the UKRAINE was depleted of the ROYAL FAMILIES who had wandered off to the BALKANS, ITALY, FRANCE, SPAIN and NORTH AFRICA.

So, the messengers were charged with finding a RIC or ROYAL FAMILY and they found one in RURIC who accepted the offer and his entire family moved to NOVHOROD and from there to KIYIV. This family, while very numerous, was extinguished by the TARTARS and the MUSCOVITES. Only one branch survived after the massacre in NOVHOROD, first by IVAN III, and then by IVAN THE TERRIBLE. The traitor: ALEXANDER NEVSKY was the only Prince ever to be OUTCAST by the NOVGORODIANS, when he urged them to make an alliance with the TARTARS. And, the last descendent of Alexander Nevsky was IVAN THE TERRIBLE himself!

Ivan III ruled from 1462 to 1505 as Grand Duke. He married Zoe, a niece of the Byzantine Emperor. Therefore, he declared that Moscow was "The Third Rome," and a forth Rome will not happen. He further declared that all titles in RUS can not exceed the titles in Moscow, both in the past or present or the future. Thus, all Ukrainian Kings were demoted to princes. Finally, he decreed that Muscovy will be the protector of ORTHODOXY. Also, he stopped making tribute payments to the Tartars but send them presents instead, while keeping all tribute payments for himself.

Peter I (The Great) ruled from 1689 to 1725. Peter called his country ROSSIA, it is still called that by the natives to this day. The word Russia was coined by Voltaire, who was hired to write the definitive History of Russia according to the specifications provided by Catherine II (The Great).

Peter is credited with many innovations, which were all made by Leibnitz. First, Peter wanted a new language (he wanted to get away from Ukrainian. Initially, he wanted to use Dutch. But, his advisors advised against it, because otherwise they could not raid the Ukrainian treasures of Literature, Music and Art. Thus Peter modified the alphabet slightly: some letters were deleted for example i, h and all umlauts for a, e, i, o, u. In Ukrainian the umlaut is pronounced as a "Y" prefix. Thus, ï is pronounced yi. Thus the spelling of Kiïb in the cyrillic, is pronounced Kiyiv in latin. And, the very important "TABLE OF RANKS" comes directly from Leibnitz with all German names and prefixes: Feldwebel and unter and ober.

It should be noted that Western Historians were always antagonistic toward the East, in particular against ORTHODOXY. In order for the Pope to rule Christendom the rival in Constantinople had to be defeated first, only then could the Orthodox Christians be converted to Catholicism. And, as you add more Catholics, more money flown into the Catholic church.

Therefore western historians wrote history as if they conducted "warfare." Everyone knows that when you conduct warfare you "DIVIDE and CONQUER." Therefore, eastern culture, geography, language and political subdivision is fragmented into the smallest minutia possible and a perverted version of history is taught.

***

Suddenly our train came to a halt. It was dawn. A conductor came and told us we had to get out. The tracks were destroyed that night by a massive raid on COTTBUS. We had to take trucks, which were waiting for us and pass through the city to the other side where the tracks were still intact and from there the train would take us directly to BERLIN.

So, we boarded our designated truck and soon our column moved down the road. Within minutes we drove through COTTBUS. The town was leveled. I did not see a single building standing as we drove through the heart of the town. Instead there were only smoldering ruins and a foul smell of death. Maria sat next to Emilia, so Emilia took out a handkerchief and covered her eyes. This was not a pretty sight...

We arrived at the train station on the other end of town. It was intact, pretty as a picture and clean as a whistle. We found the track on which our train would take us to Berlin. We settled down on our baggage and all of a sudden everybody was hungry. So, Emilia took out a loaf of butter, a bag of sugar and made "sweet sugar balls." I had a few and I could not eat any more. I needed bread...

While everybody ate the butter balls, I decided to scout the platform. So, I quietly walked up the platform. And, there I saw what I needed... A few soldiers munching away at some bread. I moved closer and stared at the bread... One of the soldiers noticed me. He said: "Willst Du ein stück Brot?" I said nothing, I just stared at the bread. Then he laughed and handed me the unfinished portion, practically a half a loaf of bread. I mustered one of the few words I knew. I said: "Danke." And, holding on to the bread for dear life I ran back to my family.I handed the bread to Emilia and she laced into me: "Where did you get it?" I pointed to the soldiers and she waved them a "thank you." They waved back and laughed...

Now we could eat as far as I was concerned. Emilia divided the bread equally among the six of us, and now we had bread, butter and some sugar sprinkled on it. What a fabulous meal...

As the dusk set in our train arrived. We loaded our baggage in our designated compartment and we were off, once again to Berlin. I fell asleep as soon as the train started rolling...
When the train stopped again, we were in BERLIN.

We arrived at the main station, smack in the center of town. Emilia got a porter and said only one word: "TAXI." The porter took our luggage and led the way. He found us a taxi and Emilia tipped him. He was very thankful, apparently the Germans are not great tippers. He loaded our luggage and we were ready to go to the "Meldesamt," Emilia's and George's reporting office.

But, before we could leave a SCHUPO, a policeman, noticed our motley group. He came up to Emilia and said, "Ausweis bitte." Emilia gave him the her MARSCHBEFEHL. He examined it and asked for more ID. She gave him her passport. He looked at it and said: "Hm, Volksdeutche?" Then, he turned to George and asked for his ID. George gave him his passport. He looked at it carefully, then said: "Hm, OSTLAND." Then he let us go. So, even though Emilia and George were married, Emilia was a second class human, while George belonged to an even lower class.

Then we were off. What a beautiful city I thought. Shops everywhere. And, every shop with a magnificent display window. The streets were whistle clean, not a speck of dust anywhere!

The taxi driver took us down a beautiful boulevard and finally he stopped. Emilia and George dashed out, while the rest of us waited in the taxi. Within a few minutes, Emilia and George reappeared and we were off to our new home.

We were assigned a beautiful apartment right next to the TIERGARTEN (ZOO), which was a beautiful park, and which flaunted a superb Zoo. Our apartment had three rooms, a kitchen and a bathroom. So, Emilia and George shared one room, Maria and Grandma another, while Emma and I shared the third. It was a second floor walkup in a what appeared to me a four story building. Emilia and George had to report for work in three days, so a few days were given to setup house. And we did...

Everything was wonderful, except I missed my favorite bed above the ever warm oven...

The Occupation of Kiyiv

THE GERMAN OCCUPATION of KIYIV lasted from September 1941 to October 1943.

When the Germans invaded the SOVIET Union on June 22, 1941, the Soviets were totally unprepared to give them any resistance. In fact, Stalin thought that this was only some sort of exercise of Germany. But, within a few days it became crystal clear that an allout invasion of the SOVIET UNION was in progress. In total, nearly 300 motorized divisions or about 6 million Germans and their allies were invading the Soviet Union from the West and the North, Norway and Finland. Again, as during the time of Napoleon PRACTICALLY ALL OF EUROPE was invading "Mother Russia." Only PORTUGAL, Great BRITAIN, SWITZERLAND, POLAND, SWEDEN, SERBIA, DENMARK and GREECE did not sent contingents in this all out attack, all other countries of Europe did!

Of course Napoleon invaded with only 600,000 Frenchmen and allies, of which only 5,000 saw Paris again. However, this was different. German armor had crushed Poland, France, Denmark and Norway. While Poland was erased from the map of Europe, France and Norway became staunch allies of HITLER. So, it is not surprising that Stalin was not only in a state of shock, but sheer panic raged throughout the STALIN empire.

Just a few years before the invasion STALIN had purged the entire military leadership in the SOVIET UNION. Very few generals survived that purge. And, for good measure, about 75% of the officer corps were purged with them. The highest ranking general, at that time was

VLASSOV, the darling of STALIN. And, he was recalled to MOSCOW to organize the defense against the Finns and Norwegians who were pressing on Moscow. So, while VLASSOV organized the defense of Moscow, Stalin and all his cronies fled to the hinterlands.

In the Ukraine, STALIN's last reign of terror, 1936 to 1939 was still fresh on everybody's mind. And, practically every Ukrainian preferred fighting with the Germans against Stalin, rather than the other way around.

Meanwhile, during the preceding era of WARCOMMUNISM, from about 1923 to 1933, such an invasion was not ruled out. In fact, during that time defensive lines were formed to protect for such an eventuality. But, the partition of POLAND, shifted the new borders of the SOVIET UNION and there was not enough time to build defensive pockets in the new areas. At the same time, the prior defensive perimeters were sorely neglected as seasoned soldiers were replaced with recruits.

Kiyiv, was originally an ANCHOR in that defensive line. But, at the time of the German invasion, it was practically depleted of all the armor and personnel. So, a new army was quickly raised in July, with KHRUSHCHEV as its commissar. But, as the GERMANS approached, most of the recruits simply VANISHED and the army disintegrated practically as soon as it was formed. And, the remainder simply surrendered to the Germans, practically without a fight. Of course, STALIN would not accept that his empire was turning against him, while the Germans, eager for another victory called every surrender of a SOVIET army, a victory. Thus, the first Battle for KIYIV, was not a battle at all. Yet our history books call it a battle, simply because Stalin and Hitler called it that.

In any event, officially the battle for KIYIV was over by September 20, 1941, and within a few days the victorious Germans marched into Kiyiv. There, they were treated as liberators, as women and children lined the streets and showered the GERMAN WEHRMACHT with flowers, offering them bread and salt.

Emilia had our house boarded up, rented a flat in the center of Kiyiv and we moved there. The reason being: It was safer to be a part of the inconspicuous crowd than to stick out like a sour thumb in suburbia. But, when her husband was murdered we returned to the house. At that point she simply did not care.

As soon as the Germans settled in KIYIV, they began THEIR reign of terror. While the Ukrainians wanted to be their allies, the Germans did not want them at all. All of continental EUROPE was allied with Germany at that time. Instead, they had in mind to enslave the Ukrainians and all EASTERNERS for that matter, to work on their farms and in their industries as OSTARBEITERS. So, as soon as they settled in, they began rounding up all the young folks and deported them to GERMANY.

Their method was always the same. They would surround the market place. Then, the SS would move in and make the arrests. JEWS and GYPSIES of all ages were arrested, detained and then they simply disappeared, while all others between the ages of 16 to 26 were detained and usually shipped off to GERMANY. Emilia was arrested twice, but managed to extricate herself each time.

Meanwhile, the Germans formed a new Government in Kiyiv. They preferred for the locals to run the daily affairs, while they remained the superiors in each department, in the background. Thus, the appearance was that the Ukrainians governed themselves.

It was no secret to our neighbors that EMILIA was part German. Her father was Grotte who changed his name to a russian name. At first, delegations of neighbors began arriving begging her to take a post with the new administration, but each time she refused. Her argument was that, she was not a political animal, and politics to her was dirty business. But, the delegations kept on coming and coming and coming... They refused to take her no for an answer. And, in the end, she agreed to seek an administrative post. When she applied, she was immediately made the assistant to the local MAYOR, Dr. BAGAZIL in the Kuriniv district of KIYIV.

So, for about 8 hours of the day "I WAS IN CHARGE" of our "MINI FARM." I was thrilled. I had all the animals to myself and the full run of the primary property. But, I was not allowed to go to our second property across the YAR. And, I never did. That is, while Emma attended school and Emilia was on her new job.

However, this arrangement did not last too long. Emilia found a "KINDERGARTEN" which, according to her, was just right for me. So, one day I was taken to this morbid place. And, I did not like it at all. First, I told her outright. But, she would not hear of it. So, I decided to become so unruly in that "morgue," that they would not keep me. This was the only time I disagreed with Emilia and did something about it. The upshot was, I was allowed to stay at home with our animals, and I was allowed to take care of them.

Of course, my biggest helper and protector was FUZZY (our St. Bernard). We had initially about 5 pigs and 10 piglets, but the Germans "arrested" two pigs and five piglet; then, we had a flock of geese, about 12 of them, and that flock was decimated by the Germans to six; then we had a whole bunch of chickens, about 20 and there the Germans arrested about 10, but they let us keep our RED ROOSTER, who was a certified champion. Finally, they let us keep our GOAT, which was "MY GOAT." That is, when I was much smaller, I was a sickly fellow. Practically every childhood disease paid me a visit. And, to top it off, I developed an allergy to cow's milk. So, my father went to a fair and bought a champion goat, just for me. That goat was supposed to give 20 liters (quarts) of milk EVERY DAY. But, after we put her on a small pasture and tried to milk her, she gave less than a pint! So, what happened? Well, the goat liked to suckle herself and by the time we came to milk her, there was hardly anything left. Eventually, Emilia found a way to wean her off her habit. And, when the Germans occupied KIYIV, my goat yielded her full quota. The goat, and our supply in the cellar became our survival food. The only thing I lacked was BREAD. So, I waited up for Emilia each evening for the bread she would bring, and she never disappointed me.

When Emilia built her house, she had the foresight to build a huge oven in one room. The oven occupied practically the whole room. This was her bakery and cookery, all rolled into one. The oven had a huge platform on top, which could easily sleep six grownups or more. This is where I made my bed. The oven was still warm in the evening from Emilia's morning cooking and baking. Before she would go to work, she always cooked something for me and my sister Emma. I loved that place. Emilia put a few layers of padding on top of that oven and topped them with sheets and a down comforter, thus it was like a regular bed but, much cozier and warmer. In addition, the room had one window, and when darkness fell, I would crawl into that bed and peek out the window for Emilia's return. And, when she returned from work, I would get a slice of dark bread, break it up into small pieces into a bowl and poor some goat milk over it. This was ambrosia for me.

Thus, we settled into a routine. Then, one day EMILIA took me aside and asked me if I could keep a secret. Of course, I could, I assured her. So, she told me that we might have a few visitors staying in our attic, but this would be only temporary anyway. And, from then on, practically each day, a few visitors would arrive and make themselves at home in our attic. Eventually, Emilia housed up to 20 visitors. These, were all young people, targeted by the GERMANS for deportation who needed a temporary hideout until they could find safer quarter. To tell you the truth, I hardly noticed them, they made no noise at all. In this way Emilia saved literally hundreds of lives.

However, towards the end of 1942, one group, after studying our routine, came at night, when we were away from the house, killed FUZZY who was chained during the night and robbed us of everything that was not nailed down in the house. The moral of this story is: NO GOOD DEED GOES UNPUNISHED. Much later, however, when we were already in GERMANY, Emilia met one of the perpetrators. He was very ashamed for what he and his companions did. He asked her for forgiveness and EMILIA forgave.

So, while the house was full of visitors in the attic, I ruled in our garden. All animals respected me, especially when FUZZY was by my side. But, one gander had it in for me. Sometimes he would break out and attack me. When I had Fuzzy on my side this was no problem, FUZZY would chase him away and I would lock him up with his flock. But, sometimes FUZZY was not by my side, then the only evasive action I had, was to lay flat on the ground, cover my face the best I could and let them peck away at me. Then, FUZZY would rush in, chase them away and we would lock them up. In any event, I never had a dull moment in our yard.

Then, on one gorgeous day in the early spring of 1942, there was a ring at our front gate. I opened the gate to a tiny crack. There were two GERMAN soldiers. They were very friendly and wanted to get in. So, I let them in, even though I had strict orders not to let anyone in. But, who could argue with soldiers, especially when I could not understand them. So, they came in, walked around Emilia's fruit trees and then made signs that they needed a saw and a shovel. So, I took them to our barn and they picked up some tools. I thought for sure, they were going to "arrest" a few trees and berry bushes, I tried to tell them that we already GAVE, our livestock was decimated and we were officially allowed to keep the remainder. I am sure they did not understand me, they only grinned and made some comforting gestures. Then, they took some tools and went to EMILIA's orchard. There, they proceeded to prune the trees. Then, they fertilized the trees until the entire orchard was put in tip top shape. And, if that was not enough, they proceeded to trim and fertilize our berry bushes. They worked like demons, and by the end of the day Emilia's orchard and berry bushes were all in tip top shape. When evening fell, they washed up at our well, said: "AUF WIEDERSEHN" and left. I could not believe the whole incident. And, when EMILIA came home from work, I told her everything. She was stunned. Next morning, after she had done all her baking and cooking she went out into her garden to inspect their handy work. She came back sobbing, she did not expect this kindness. She truly appreciated their labor.

As it turned out, they were "farm boys" from the Black Forest area. They were on leave and strolled down our street when they noticed Emilia's orchard. So, they decided to take a closer look. And, when they found that the orchard was magnificent but begging for work, they decided to do the work right then and there. They came back a few more times and this time I would let them in without hesitation. This only goes to prove that among all people there are some good ones left and there is no need to despair of humanity, even though a handful villains grab the limelight and our attention.

Proskurov

So, finally we were on our way. By now trains moved only by night because the air was now dominated by Soviet planes and they strafed anything that moved West: Trains, cars and even horse and buggy. Then, at dawn our train stopped quite suddenly and we were told to disembark. We were in the midst of a dense forest, well camouflaged from any air attack.

We travelled through an area which is now called the "epicenter of the Trypillian" culture. That is, an area which can best be described by drawing a line from Kiyiv to Lviv, the capital of Galicia. Then, using the center of that line draw a circle, including Kiyiv and Lviv. That area was studded with mounds which have been recently excavated.

The excavations have yielded pottery dating back to 5000 BC.
That is, before the pyramides were built in Egypt. And, it has been proven that the pottery of the Trypillian culture was the forerunner to the ancient Greek pottery.

The Ukrainian Museum in New York City has a comprehensive brochure depicting that pottery. In any case, the Trypillian area was very important in history. This is where the GOTHS gathered for their "Allthing," a general meeting which often determined some "massive action." For example: Aleric gathered the Goths here. He was elected King and invaded from there the Roman Empire to liberate the Goths who were mistreated by the Roman Empire, about 400 AD. He liberated the Goths and became the highest ranking ROMAN official, "Master of the Horse." This enabled him to arm all Goths and seek a new homeland for them. They moved into Italy, sacked Rome and moved south to seek passage to North Africa. By then, other Goths had settled near Cartage. But, as fate would have it, he died and the remaining Goths buried him with his treasure in the Busento River. Then, they abandoned his plan and decided to join up with other Goths in France and Spain.

Why did they do all that?

Well, when the Roman Empire accepted Christianity by Constantine, it was the ARIAN form, from Bishop Arius. And, for the first 70 years Arian Christianity was the norm. But then, about 375 AD, the Roman Empire changed the Christian view. That is, ATHANASIUS prevailed and ORTHODOXY became the dominant form of Christianity. Thus, Arian Christians became heretics and as such they were hunted down, killed and their property taken, according to the teachings of St. Augustine.

Then, in 396 the Huns invaded Europe. They defeated the Alans and then the Goths, and millions of Goths sought refuge in the Roman Empire. Some were allowed to cross the Danube and were promised good land to farm in the Balkans, while another million or so moved West. They crossed the Rhine River and settled in Southern Gaul, near Bordeaux. But, in the Balkans the GOTHS were virtually imprisoned and mistreated by the Roman Empire. So, when word reached the remaining Goths in their homeland about their lot, Alaric gathered the Goths and set out to liberate them.

At that time the Huns, allied with the Germans and Burgundians ravaged the Roman Empire from Gaul to the Balkans, despite the fact that Constantinople paid them a massive annual tribute not to violate their Empire. And, when Attila became their leader, and received a marriage proposal by Honoria, the sister of the Roman Emperor Valentinian III which Valentinian refused to honor, Attila decided to conquer Gaul.

Thus, he raised a massive army and invaded Gaul. But, in 451, the newly settled Goths, Alans and Scythians rose to the occasion and defended the Empire. They met at CHALON SUR MARNE and in that epic battle the Huns, Germans and Burgundians were defeated. However, the impotent Roman Empire was not able to finish off the Huns. Why?

Well, before Christianity, Rome could flaunt some 52 legions stationed throughout their empire. But, after accepting Christianity they could not muster enough soldiers to guard the Emperor, much less to defend the Empire. That is, Roman citizens prepared themselves for the second coming of Christ. They became monks and priests while soldiering was entirely abandoned. It was more important to save the SOUL rather than the FLESH. In fact, even the Imperial Guard was filled with VARANGIAN GOTHS. So, the Roman Empire embarked on a new mode of operation: Entire nations were hired to do the fighting for them. Thus, when Attila died, his three sons were encouraged to fight among themselves for supremacy, and they nearly exterminated each other. Then, the GEPID Goths were hired to finish off the Huns, which they did. But, when the Gepids became too mighty for the Roman Empire, they hired the AVARS to destroy the GEPIDS, which they did. Now, Avars raided and plundered the Roman Empire. Then, to protect Italy from the constant raids of the Germans, Burgundians and Avars, the OSTOGOTHS were hired to settle in ITALY, which they did with their King THEODORIC. The rule of the Ostogoths gave Italy decades of peace and prosperity. But, because the Ostogoths were Arian Christians this remained an irreconcilable issue. And, when Theodoric died, the Emperor Justinian seized that occasion to evict the Ostrogoths. That "civil war" lasted nearly 50 years, and while the Ostogoths were eventually expelled and joined their kinfolk in Gaul and Spain, Italy was again left ravaged and devastated.

Finally, to prevent another incursion by the Goths, the Roman Empire changed the name of the Goths remaining in their homeland to SLAVS, cutting the umbilical cord to the Goths in Gaul and Spain, to prevent other wars of liberation. Thus, practically overnight the name was changed from Goths to Slavs, and practically overnight the SLAVS appeared on the European historical scene. (The fact that the Goths and Slavs had merged in antiquity, before the Trojan war, into one nation by exchanging their kings was conveniently brushed aside).

Meanwhile, this turmoil and the inability to protect the citizens was seized by the Bishop of Rome, once he found a suitable protector, Charlemagne. Thus, in 800 AD, a concordat was reached between the Bishop of Rome and Charlemagne: The Bishop of Rome would "elevate" himself to the leader of Christianity calling himself POPE and would elevate the King of the Franks, Charlemagne, to Emperor provided he defended the new faith and the Papacy in perpetuity, and a new Roman Empire was formed. We call it today the HOLY ROMAN EMPIRE.

Meanwhile, this CONCORDAT is called the GERMAN CONCORDAT, to distinguish it from the French CONCORDAT reached by FRANCIS I and the ITALIAN CONCORDAT reached by MUSSOLINI.

Thus, the Germans became the first conquistadors of Europe.

They protected the Pope and in return they had a free hand in dealing with the "infidels" in Europe and became the DESIGNATED RULERS throughout Europe.

Now CHARLEMAGNE took on the Avars, but he could not defeat them. So, to finish off the Avars, the Magyars were invited to exterminate them. And, the Magyars came and with the help of the LANGOBARDS, exterminated the Avars, and now THEY raided the Roman Empire.

But in 955, the Western Emperor Otto I defeated the Magyars at Lechfeld and the Magyars accepted Christianity from Rome. Thus, they became "legitimate" residents of Europe, with a new name called "Hungarians." The German historian MOMMSON calls this "Völkerwanderung," (Nationwandering), as if these nations meandered through Europe without cause or without purpose. But, he needed to leave this impression in order that Germany could draw on these nations for their own identity. Hitler called it: "KULURKAMPF," the rape of other cultures to suit Germany.

***

We waited out the entire day, before we were allowed to embark the train. As soon as the dark set in the train began to roll west. I fell asleep practically instantly. Iwoke up when the train came to a screeching halt. A conductor was running down the track yelling to get off the train, and we did. What happened was, the track in front of us was blown up, presumably by partisans. In any event, we were called to a meeting.

There, the conductor explained that the track was damaged and that PROSKUROV was only a few miles away. We had an option, to stay with the train until the track was fixed or to walk to Proskurov where another train would take us to Berlin. So, Emilia, George and Anna talked this over and we decided to walk to Proskurov since the train was a sitting duck in case of an air attack. We took our baggage and started to walk along the track. We seemed to walk forever. Emilia led our group, followed by George and Anna, then Maria and me, while Emma brought up the rear. We walked, and we walked, and we walked...

Then, we came to a crossing and we saw trucks. Emilia flagged down a truck and asked for a ride to the train station, and the kind driver agreed to take our motley group there. When we arrived at the station, it was totally bombed out, at least so it seemed to me. But, the station master assured us that by next morning the trains would be running again. But, now I got terribly sick. I was coughing and was running a fever. Emilia examined me and determined I had pneumonia. So, I had to be hospitalized. And, without much ado I was taken to the hospital. Of course, my sickness changed everything. We had to stay put for a few weeks. Then, Emilia disappeared and returned with a big grin on her face. So, what happened?

Proskurov was a major railroad junction and a major supply depot for the GERMAN WEHRMACHT. In charge of it was a GERMAN MAJOR who had shot himself accidentally while cleaning his revolver. Usually, this was not a serious matter but on that day Hitler had issued new orders that anyone maiming himself in order to avoid being sent to the front was to be shot on the spot. So, if the Major went to the local hospital, his gunshot wound would be reported and he faced very serious consequences. When Emilia went to the "Arbeitsamt" to change her "Marschbefehl" and it was found out that she had a medical degree and was an agronomist to boot she was immediately sent to the Major. She cleaned and dressed his wound and was offered an immediate job, reporting directly to him. This gave her privileged quarters, rations and pay. We landed in paradise!

The Major was a real "MENSCH" and treated Emilia with kid gloves. In fact, he began courting her when he found out that George was a "distant relative." This put Emilia into a situation she could not handle properly. So, in order to resolve this Gordon knot, she decided to marry George while he adopted me and Emma.

Eventually, our stay in Paradise had to come to an end. By November the front was less than 30 miles away. So, Emilia secured new marching orders. But this time we travelled in style, in a regular passenger car with our own compartment. Before we departed the Major gave us a whole list of friends and relatives in Berlin and elsewhere, and urged Emilia to turn to them whenever she was in need...

Kursk and its aftermath

The battle of Kursk was the decisive battle of WWII. After that battle the German WEHRMACHT was unable to launch another major offensive in the East. It is significant because of a number of reasons:

1. The battle took place in JULY, thus dispelling the notion that GENERAL WINTER was RUSSIA's greatest general.

2. The combatants were nearly equal in numbers, dispelling the notion that the Russians needed a numerical superiority to defeat the Germans. In fact, until the battle of Kursk the Soviets were outnumbered in every major battle where the Germans were defeated: Leningrad, Moscow and Stalingrad.

    * At Leningrad, the entire might of the WEHRMACHT was unable to take the city. The siege lasted 900 days. And, eventually the Germans, French, Spanish, Fins and Norwegians were defeated there.

    * At Moscow, Vlasov created a rag tag army mostly from political prisoners and regulars and pushed back the Germans along the ENTIRE FRONT from 125 to 300 miles, depending on the sector. There the Germans outnumbered Vlasov by more than 2 to 1. There, the Germans lost 95% of their armor!
    Army Group North was essentially eliminated for any offensive for the rest of the war.

    * At Stalingrad, the Germans outnumbered the defenders by more than 3 to 1, yet the best army in the WEHRMACHT

120

was unable to rout the defenders. And, when for the first time the SOVIETS had the numerical superiority, during the counteroffensive, they destroyed 4 armies: Two Romanian armies, one Hungarian Army, one Italian army and captured whatever remained from the German 6th army; 120,000 Germans went into SOVIET captivity and only 3,000 returned home when the war was over.

* At Kursk, the number of combatants was nearly 2 million on each side, making it the largest land battle ever fought in Europe, dwarfing the battle of CHALONS SUR MARNE by nearly 1 million total combatants. (This is when the VISIGOTHS, ALANS and SCYTHIANS defended the WEST against Attila the Hun in 451, who's allies were the OSTROGOTHS, BURGUNDIANS and GERMANS). And, when the dust settled at Kursk, the Germans had lost 2,000 airplanes, 3,000 tanks and over 20,000 heavy guns. This armor alone could not be replaced and thus GERMANY was doomed from then on.

What is interesting is that, just before the Battle of Kursk Hitler approached Stalin for a negotiated peace. But, when Molotov and von Ribbentrop met, the Germans wanted all the territories they occupied at that time, while Molotov wanted the borders before the German invasion. Thus, the conference proved to be fruitless and the armor had to decide the fate of the Germans. And, when CHURCHILL found out about that conference, he called for a conference with STALIN and ROOSEVELT, which was eventually held in DECEMBER of 1943 in TEHERAN. This was the first 3 Power conference. There, Churchill got a promise from STALIN not to accept any GERMAN peace terms, short of UNCONDITIONAL SURRENDER! STALIN agreed to that conference because by then he had the GERMANS on the run and the WEST could not afford to lose such a valuable ally.

Of course, today, we call it the "third' expansion of "Western Europe" into the East. The first was by Charlemagne to the river Elbe, with a demilitarized zone "Brandenburg" on the right bank.

The second was by Napoleon who expanded Western Europe to include Poland. In honor of his love Maria Walevska. Thus, the third expansion was by Hitler, to include the Ukraine, Byelorussia and the Baltic states. (For some reason the expansion of the Teutonic Knights is not counted, and thus we forget that the Teutonic Knights conquered the Slavic Prussians, took their name and became the "landed nobility in Germany." The titles they gave themselves were "Junkers and von."

3. The mystique of GERMAN armor and technology. Three SOVIET weapons proved to be decisive in the war and were never duplicated by Germany even though they tried: The T/34 tank; the KATJUSHA rocket launcher and the sub machine gun.

When the T/34 was first encountered, it was misused by the SOVIETS, it was used as a SINGLE FORTRESS. The T/34 was a medium tank yet outperformed much heavier tanks in the German arsenal, because of its sloped armor. Thus, German tanks attacked it only in a WOLFPACK, with 10 or more German tanks. And, after 12 to 20 hits the T/34 was eventually destroyed. But, in practically every encounter, the T/34 took 3 to 4 German tanks with it. Still, the Germans considered the tank too bulky. But, when ZHUKOV changed the strategy from a SINGLE FORTRESS to TANK FORMATIONS, employing 10 or more T/34's, they turned the German tanks, TIGERS and LEOPARDS, into SCHROTT.

B. The KATJUSHA rocket was a GERMAN nemesis. It was mounted on a truck. It fired 10 to 20 salvos of 24 missiles and moved into a new position. Thus, German guns could not zero in on the location of a specific launcher. This rocket launcher, the Germans tried to duplicate. But, they could not. Because, each time they would fire a salvo, the truck would explode from the vibrations. Of course, eventually "German technology" would have figured out the problem of RESONANCE but, until the end of the war they could not. Instead they developed a "Nebelwerfer," a single shot rocket launcher.

C. To the GERMANS, the RIFLE was standard equipment for the foot soldier. While their rifle was more accurate, the submachine gun was deadlier in close combat. It could fire 10 times the bullets of a conventional rifle. And, in some situation, such as trench warfare the rifle could be more effective and more economical but, it was nearly useless in close combat.

Thus, INNOVATION was on the SOVIET side and the BATTLE   of KURSK proved it beyond any doubt for all rational people.

D. At the beginning of the war the German Air Force was supreme. But, by the time of Stalingrad, the Soviets achieved parity. And, after the Battle of Kursk, Soviet planes dominated the skies with Migs. When the Korean war started, the Soviets had air superiority. It took American ingenuity to beat them at their game.

E. Last but not least. In 1941, 1942 and 1943 Stalin asked for a "SECOND FRONT." However, Churchill was against engaging the Germans for fear of another "DUNQUERQE."

Stalin, however, knew after the battle of Kursk that he did not need the allies to defeat Germany. Thus, instead of launching his forces against Berlin, he negotiated with FDR that Berlin was his for the taking and used 1944 to secure Soviet domination in the Balkans, Kurland and Poland.

Now it was the Allies who clamored for an invasion of France, because otherwise the Soviets would not only defeat Germany, but also take over France, Spain and Italy. At that point, with the Soviets on the Channel the threat to England loomed to be larger than ever. Thus, D Day was launched to save France and not to defeat Germany. The slogan "to defeat Germany" was just that, a slogan.

Germany was defeated after the Battle of Kursk. The Germans knew it, that is why they tried to assassinate Hitler in 1944. Too bad that America was lured into this adventure by

Churchill. Too bad that America lost so many lives in the last year of the war to save France. Had D Day been launched in January or February of 1945, many American lives would have been saved.

*   ***

George was enamored by the German armor and believed their propaganda. Thus, when the Battle of KURSK started, he was certain that German armor would crush the Soviets once and for all. Emilia was not so sure and just to be on the safe side she asked for and received a MARSCHBEFEHL to BERLIN. That is, now she and her family were allowed to leave KIYIV and move to BERLIN.

During that time George became a frequent visitor. I was very impartial to him. Not that I disliked him, I did not. But, in my book he was quite useless. The simplest chores around our mini farm were major obstacles to him. Instead, I really liked another visitor EMILIA had: NICK RODALITZKY. First of all, each time Nick visited us, he brought me a present. And, no matter how small it was, it was HUGE to me because I felt appreciated.

Secondly, he treated me like an "adult." That is, he talked to me and shared my concerns: The animals, the fruit trees and our crop. Therefore, I always thought of him as a PRACTICAL man. Finally, he gave me a nickname: TOTOSHA, while EMMA got the nickname KOKOSHA. So, whenever he came he would start with: "And how is TOTOSHA and KOKOSHA today..."

Nick did not believe in the German propaganda either and he too got a MARSCHBEFEHL to Berlin. As soon as the outcome of the battle became known, Emilia made the final preparations to leave KIYIV. The livestock and most of our possessions were given away to relatives and friends. Emilia kept one pig which was slaughtered and cooked. Then, Emilia packed all the essentials for our journey into knapsacks, mostly bacon slabs from the slaughtered pig, butter and sugar. She prepared a knapsack for each one of us. It contained one pair of shoes, one pair of underwear, one shirt or blouse, the rest was all food: Bacon slabs, butter and sugar. Notice, socks were a luxury in the UKRAINE and seldom used. Instead, a wrap or newspaper was used. In addition, Emilia packed four suitcases, two for herself and two smaller ones for Emma.

George argued that German armor would be victorious and urged EMILIA to bury all valuables. So, Emilia and George dug a hole behind our barn and buried our valuables there: A huge SAMOVAR, an antique RECORD PLAYER and about six suitcases loaded with our worldly possessions. Then, one day George came to EMILIA and pleaded with her to take him and his family with him on EMILIA's MARSCHBEFEHL. In his overconfidence he did not secure a MARSCHBEFEHL, and without one he and his family were doomed to stay in Kiyiv. Emilia agreed and had him and his family added as "DISTANT RELATIVES." So, according to EMILIA, on October 23, 1943 we left our home for the last train to BERLIN: EMILIA, ANNA (George's mother), George, Emma, Maria (Masha) and I. And, as we were leaving for good, I was sure that as soon as we turned the corner of our street, our neighbors dug up our possessions and must have had a few chuckles. (Kiyiv was taken by the Soviets November 6, 1943).

The last train to BERLIN was a freight train. An endless number of train cars carried away whatever was not nailed down from the Ukraine. We were assigned an open car which carried nails. We huddled in one corner of the car, with the adults forming a circle, while Masha and I were in the center. By the time the train began to move, it was dark and we could see the streaks of distant shells and the faint thunder of the guns. The second Battle of Kiyiv had just started...

Human Toll

How do we reconcile the carnage of the great wars? How do we measure the human toll? Let us begin with World War II and let the basis be von Clausewitz's "ON WAR."

One way is to go to the encyclopedia and look up the casualties each nation sustained. If one were to do that, we would find some amazing results. I have chosen to use the data published by the "Encyclopedia Britannica" of 1962. Why 1962? Simple, it shows the British propaganda in its most convoluted way, in a way which is most favorable to England. Examine the conclusion on pages 799 to 801 in volume 23.

First, we notice there is no "breakdown" by nationality for WW II. Why is that? [The carnage of World War I, Table I on page 716 in the same volume has a summary by nationality.]

The reason is quite obvious, most casualties of the Western European countries resulted from actions at the EASTERN FRONT. These countries were allies of Germany for the only adversary Germany and her allies fought on the Eastern front was our ally the Soviet Union. This, however, would make them our enemies. But since we do not want to flaunt the extent of their involvement against the Allied powers, we omit their casualties! Thus, the "books" imply that Albania, Austria, Bohemia, Bulgaria, Croatia, Estonia, Finland, France, Latvia, Lithuania, Moravia, Netherlands, Norway, Rumania, Slovakia, Slovenia and Spain were our allies, not Germany's. IS THAT NOT CORRECT?

This brings us to the last paragraph under World War II, entitled "The Cost." There, we are provided with a descriptive summary for the nation's losses. Of course, only the "major" belligerent are listed. This veils the multitude of nations involved in the war, and at the same time, misrepresents the nearly even carnage on both sides (as expected according to von Clausewitz). The summary accounts for only the dead, not the maimed, not the wounded, as if their suffering can be taken for granted.

Since von Clausewitz is considered to be the authority on modern warfare, we will estimate the omitted data using his reasoning. (1) According to him, once the element of surprise is lost and the war is lost, casualties will be "nearly equal." This is so because the "retribution" principle works against the aggressor and total casualties are "equalized." (2) He provides an estimate of the wounded, based on the actual casualties. On average, there are five wounded for each killed in action. We will use only three to be conservative. Finally, his "theory" applies only to continental Europe, where retribution is possible. Below are the tabulated results in the chart form in the order of the paragraph's summary:

1) United States of America................... 292,100 lives.
2) British Commonwealth..................... 544,596 lives.
3) Soviet Union................................... 7,500,000 lives.
4) France.. 210,671 lives.
5) Germany .... 2,850,000 lives. ***
6) Italy.. 300,000 lives.
7) China .... 2,200,000 lives.
8) Japan .... 1,506,000 lives.
9) Total Allied casualties...................... 10,650,000 lives.
10) Total Axis casualties....................... 4,650,000 lives.
11) Total monetary cost to US .... 350 billion dollars.

On the surface, the numbers appear to be consistent. We add the Axis belligerent, Germany, Italy and Japan, and get 4,656,000 lives. (While every life for the British Commonwealth and France was counted to the last man or woman, the lives of other nations were "lumped" by the thousands. Even the USA was "lumped" by the hundred's as though we do not have the actual casualty reports.

Next, we should observe a conspicuous absence of the staunch German allies: Albania, Austria, Bohemia, Bosnia, Bulgaria, Croatia, Estonia, Finland, Hungary, Latvia, Lithuania, Moravia, Netherlands, Norway, Rumania, Slovakia, Slovenia and Spain. Collectively, their casualties were much larger than the Germans! Why? This was so because their collective population was much larger than Germany, their territorial size was much larger than Germany, and in many cases their "proportional" involvement was much larger than Germany. They needed to prove to the Germans that they were "worthy" Aryans.

Let us see how large the numbers were with respect to Germany's population and then apply a proportional factor to estimate their casualties. (I will use the closest possible census which will resemble the actual 1941 figures). The figures for the population, land area and the census date are provided.

Thus, we will introduce a small error. That error will be within five percent. This is so because some data is very old and some very recent. But, since the "birthrate" was declining or zero in Western Europe, these numbers are good approximations for the period in question.

As will be seen from the figures, Hitler controlled nearly twice as many people as there were in the entire Soviet Union at that time, about 195 million. This excludes those Soviet citizens who willingly and voluntarily both fought and labored for the Axis cause, Vlasov being the primary case in point. But their casualties have to be listed on the Axis side.

For France and Italy, the statistics are shown as subtotals and no estimates of casualties are made. Since France was an ally of Germany for 3.5 years (1941 to 1944) and our ally for 2.5 years (1940, 1944 and 1945), France's casualties must be factored according to their allegiance in order that one can discern who was actually fighting for whom.

In Italy, the situation was different. When Rome was taken in June 1944 by the Allies, Italian partisans fought from then on actively against the Germans. But because Mussolini was killed in April 1945, Italian casualties are listed on the Axis side. Technically, one sixth of the Italian casualties incurred were for the Allied cause. Other German allies were the following:

Other German Allies	Population	Size	Census
Albania	278,000	2,500	'30
Austria	7,555,338	32,376	'62
Bohemia & Moravia	10,945,970	34,507	'62
Bosnia Herzegovina	2,000,000	19,768	'18
Bulgaria	8,929,332	42,823	'83
Croatia	7,000,000	44,453	'45
Estonia	1,326,413	18,353	'40
Finland	4,869,858	130,119	'84
Hungary	10,679,000	35,911	'84
Latvia	1,994,506	25,395	'39
Lithuania	2,979,070	22,959	'40
Netherlands	14,394,589	13,203	'84
Norway	4,134,353	125,051	'84
Rumania	22,600,000	91,699	'84
Slovakia	2,450,000	14,848	'62
Slovenia/Serbia	2,911,701	18,650	'10
Spain	38,219,534	194,884	'83
Other Axis allies	143,277,661	867,509	**
Germany	67,032,242	182,104	'46
Sub Total	210,309,903	867,509	**
France (Vichy & North)	54,539,000	210,033	'84
Italy	56,939,101	119,764	'83
Total Axis in Europe	320,788,004	1,187,306	**

The estimated "other" casualties (excluding Germany, France and Italy) equals the "other" Axis population divided by the German population, then multiplied by the German casualties. Thus we "prorate" the "other" casualties to be of the same ratio as the Germans. Then, we have the following:

Other Axis casualties = 143.3 / 67.0 * 2,850,000
Other Axis casualties = 6,095,597!

Now let us include Vlasov with his casualties of more than 650,000. These were all former citizens of the Soviet Union who actually died in combat for the Germans. And, we are still not yet finished. Why?

The French casualties are the total casualties for WW II. Some resulted from engaging the Germans in 1940, 1944 and 1945, while others resulted from engaging our troops when the French were fighting for the Germans. This means that from 1941 until June 1944, French losses included casualties incurred fighting against the Allies. That is, of the 6 years of the war, France fought 2.5 years for the Allies and 3.5 years for the Germans. In the absence of actual casualties for each side, let us factor their casualties according to the time involved. That is, 2.5 years divided by 6 years yields 42%. Thus, 42% of France's casualties were losses fighting for the Allies, and 58% were losses fighting for the Germans. Thus, France had 84,482 casualties fighting for the Allies and 126,189 casualties fighting for Germany!

Notice, we are still not finished. We know that Indochina had extensive casualties. We also know that in the Philippines there were also extensive casualties. (Mac Arthur had to abandon the Philippines and re group in Australia). Let us say, that the casualties were 350,000 and 200,000 respectively. Now let us total the results again, this time with the casualties adjusted properly. Then, we can see that the casualties on both sides were nearly the same! True, we had to make some estimates, but all estimates were more than reasonable.

Allied Casualties		Axis Casualties	
=================		===============	
USA	292,100	Germany	2,850,000
British	544,596	"Other"	6,095,597
Soviet	7,500,000	Vlasov	650,000
France	84,482	France	126,139
China	2,200,000	Japan	1,506,000
Indochina	350,000	Italy	300,000
Philippines	200,000		0
=======================		=====================	
Total	11,171,178	Total	11,517,736

The lopsided disparity in casualties initiated this "investigation" in the first place. The figures stated in the "Britannica" are there to confuse and to distort the real facts. As we can see, the "actual" casualties are nearly the same. In part this is so because we had to estimate our data. Now this data was "hidden" from us to whitewash the extent of the Holocaust and to veil the extent of each nation's involvement. We should remember that for each death, the wounded and maimed are at least three times the total. Thus, roughly speaking, the human toll was 20 million dead and 60 million maimed and wounded!

Now let us examine one final point. The "British" casualties are stated for ALL MEMBERS of the BRITISH COMMONWEALTH! That is, these are the "numbers" for all English colonies, including England. Let us examine England's colonies at the time of WW II. We will look only at countries with a population of 200,000 and more. Again, we will use the most current census. This time we will list the population only. Then we have the following population count in England's colonies.

Countries within the British Empire

Country Name	Population
Australia	15,276,000
Bahamas	209,505
Bahrain	350,798
Bangladesh (part of India)	87,052,024
Barbados	270,500
Basutoland	733,000
British Guiana	628,000
Brunei	200,000
Burma	35,313,905
Canada	24,907,100
Ceylon (Sri Lanka)	12,670,000
Cyprus	301,273
Egypt	46,000,000
Fiji	646,561
Gambia	695,886
Gold Coast (Ghana)	12,827,000
Hong Kong	5,313,000
India	683,810,051
Iraq	12,029,700
Ireland	3,443,405
Jamaica	2,230,000
Jordan	3,750,000
Kenya,Uganda,Tanganyika	42,750,000
Kuwait	1,910,856
Malaya (Malaysia)	15,070,000
Malta	329,189
Mauritius	969,191
Nepal	16,100,000
New Guinea	675,369
New Zealand	3,230,000

Nigeria	82,390,000
North Borneo	470,000
Northern Rhodesia	2,550,000
Nyassaland................................	2,950,000
Oman	1,500,000
Pakistan (then part of India)	88,000,000
Rhodesia	1,738,000
Sarawak....................................	975,918
Sierra Leone	3,354,000
Solomon Islands........................	258,193
Somaliland................................	640,000
Southern Rhodesia....................	4,010,000
South West Africa....................	1,039,800
Straits Settlements.....................	1,435,000
Sudan..	20,564,364
Swaziland..................................	626,000
Trinidad & Tobago...................	1,160,000
Union of South Africa..............	26,749,000
Zanzibar	354,360
===	
Total	1,270,636,948

Since England's population was then roughly 55,767,387; we can compute the percentage of English casualties with respect to the total British subjects in the Empire. That is, 55,767 divided by 1,270,637 times 100, or 4.38%. Thus, if subjects were enrolled at a uniform rate throughout the Empire, the English casualty toll was approximately 23,902! Conversely, most casualties were from India, Pakistan and Bangladesh.

Compare this toll with the American casualties! We not only paid for the war, 350 billion dollars, but we had more than 10 times the casualties of England! How much different was the outcome in World War I? Let us look at the casualties of this war. Let us list only the lives lost in combat and examine the inferences.

Again we see that the numbers are "lopsided" to begin with. We suspect that the many casualties not listed for the central powers came from areas carved out for England and France. That is, the casualties are deliberately understated for the Ottoman Empire. That is, for Iraq, Jordan, Sudan, Syria and so on. Only Turkey is listed. The other parts of the Ottoman Empire are left out to hide the partitioning of the once mighty Empire for England and France. If we were to prorate their casualties and add them to the total, we would come up again with "near" parity in casualties for the belligerent. That is, nearly 1,800,000 casualties are kept from us to warrant our fury and "just punishment" of our enemies. Below is the table of casualties.

Casualties in World War I
(As stated by 'Encyclopedia Britannica')

Allied Nations	Killed	Central Nations	Killed
USA	126,000	Germany	1,773,700
Russia	1,700,000	Austria Hungary	1,200,000
France	1,357,800	Turkey	325,000
British	908,371	Bulgaria	87,500
Italy	650,000		......
Japan	300		......
Rumania	335,706		......
Serbia	45,000		......
Belgium	13,716		......
Greece	5,000		......
Portugal	7,222		......
Montenegro	3,000		......
Total	5,152,115	Total	3,386,200

We should observe two other facts. First, Japan lost only 300 lives in the war. Yet Japan was awarded all the key islands in the Pacific to encircle America and Russia.

Second, the single largest losses of the Allies occurred in Russia. While they are grossly understated, they still show that Russia carried the major burden of the war. For that support of the Allies, Russia was dismembered and large territories were taken away from her in Europe and Asia. For example, Finland, Poland, parts of the Western Ukraine in Europe, and territories in China and Turkey.

Meanwhile, Serbia was rewarded for starting the war and a new state was created: Jugoslavia. In that new state, Serbia became the dominant partner. Only now, do we see the repercussions of this World War I merger.

Now, let me ask you a question? In WW I, why did Russia stay in the war? Czar Nicholas II stayed in the war despite the advice of his advisors. Even when Czar Nicholas abdicated, Kerensky continued with the war. The continuation of the war was the most important factor for the Revolution in Russia! Well? (So, let me give you the answer: Constantinople). That's why! How come? Russia was promised the control of Constantinople. Well, Russia has no legitimate Patriarch! That's why there is a "PUSSY REVOLUTION" in Russia today. Rock artist, mostly female, go to the Churches and Cathedrals and play rock music. Why? because the current Patriarch in Moscow is not legitimate.

There is only one legitimate Patriarchate where a Patriarch may be located and that place is in KIYIV. KIYIV is the only legitimate PATRIARCHATE.

So, how does one create a Patriarchate? There are two ways in the Orthodox faith. The first is by a decree of the ROMAN EMPEROR from Constantinople. Well, that is not possible since we don't have a Roman Emperor. The second way is by three Patriarchs who may establish a Patriarchate. Three are needed, but only two exist who could serve Russia: Jerusalem and Addis Abbeba. All other Patriarchates are controlled by Islam: Istanbul (Constantinople), Armenia, Alexandria, Aleppo, Rome (but, surely the Pope will not cooperate installing a competitor), Kiyiv (they can't use Kiyiv because by the decree of Ivan III, no title in all of RUS can be a higher than the title in Muscovy). And, these are all the possible candidates.

135

Now, if Russia were to control Constantinople, they could install a friendly Patriarch and then they would have three Patriarchs to create a Patriarchate in Moscow. (Peter the Great had the same problem and Leibnitz advised him to form a "HOLY SYNOD" and thereby control the election of the "METROPOLITAN" and give up the notion of a Patriarch!)

One more question. When and how were the REVOLUTIONARY ideas introduced into Russia?

Do you remember Napoleon and how he was defeated in Russia, at Leipzig and at Paris by RUSSIANS. Then, the Russians occupied Paris (all the officers). There the officers learned how Western government were governed, in particular the English Parliament and the French Chamber of Deputies. They brought these ideas back to Russia when they returned and the seeds were planted for the revolution of 1914!

***

As we established before, the British casualties were mostly from India, Pakistan and Bangladesh. That is, English losses were only five percent of the actual casualties claimed. Yet India, Pakistan and Bangladesh were taxed into perpetual poverty by the English for their loyal service. Thus, English losses were roughly 45,000 while our losses were 126,000! Again, "our" price for England's welfare was three times as large as theirs. For this, we are called the "dumb and bumbling" Americans by Sir Arthur Conan Doyle (1859 to 1930) or "Bubus Americanus."

Finally, let us turn our attention to the third great holocaust in Europe: The war with Napoleon. From 1800 until 1810 Napoleon ravaged Western Europe. In 1812, his "Grand Armee" was decimated in Russia. Napoleon raced back to Paris and raised more soldiers. In 1813, his new army was destroyed at Leipzig, mainly by Russians, Prussians and Austrians. In 1814, the same Russians, Prussians and Austrians occupied Paris and demanded his abdication. Napoleon abdicated. In 1815, Napoleon came back for the third time. Before he could raise an entire new army, the Russian, Prussian, Hannoverian and English forces

136

quickly converged on him in the hope of finishing him off for good. The actual size of the armies sent were as follows:

Armies Mobilized Against Napoleon in 1815
===

Russia..........................	450,000
Prussia......................	150,000
Hannoverians............	90,000
English.....................	28,000

Napoleon raced against the smallest force, hoping to destroy it before these armies could unite. Thus, he raced against the English and Hannoverians under Wellington. At Waterloo, they met and engaged in battle. As the battle progressed, the Prussians retreated just in time to Waterloo and defeated Napoleon. Yet, we claim in our history books that England saved the day for Europe. The numbers speak for themselves. It was the Germans who saved the day for Europe, not England.

Thus, in every carnage we examined, the English contributed the least to stop it, and claimed the most credit and benefit from it.

While this may be very smart from England's point of view, we as Americans must examine and evaluate our involvement with this new perspective in mind. We should not allow ourselves to be drawn into England's propaganda. America in not a part of England's expansionary policy. We must view history for what it is. Not "What England Tells Us It IS."

Khalkhin Gol

I live in paradise. I live in Florida, in a condo where everything is taken care of for a small maintenance fee. In addition, we have a heated swimming pool which I use at least for one hour each day, sometimes more. In the course of one year I seldom miss a single day of swimming. On January 2014, I got myself a "NUTRIBULLET" and my diet was complete.

I am surrounded by three shopping centers, all within walking distance. Last but not least, a myriad of restaurants flaunt their delicacies within walking distance. And, we have many "STARBUCKS" in our area. My favorite one is only a walking distance away.

When I moved to this area in 2003, I started to frequent that Starbucks. Soon I developed a small group of "history hounds." With them we discussed many aspects of history which I advocated. For example: The role of the major concordats, Rapallo land and so on. In particular how Germany came to rule all of Europe and became a nation only in 1871. How the Germans have tried ever since to recreate a "Germanic History" by spreading confusion. (No wonder that Goebbels line was: "Repeat a lie 1000 times and it becomes the truth.") How the German language was created by Goethe, Schiller and Lessing, who were all contemporaries of Napoleon. How Napoleon did more for German unification then the Germans did for themselves.

We talked about "what makes a battle significant," and how to differentiate between a "battle and a brawl." The last one was the easiest to quantify: 5 divisions. That is whenever there were less than 5 divisions involved then it was a brawl and above that made it a battle. What makes a battle significant was much harder to quantify. Eventually we settled on the significance of the battle to the outcome of the war. Thus you can clearly see that D Day was not significant to the outcome of the war in Europe; while Midway was the most important battle in the Pacific.

When we talked about World War II, everybody new about Pearl Harbor, Midway, Enola Gay and VJ day. Few knew of the battle of the Coral Sea. (It was the first battle in history where the opposing carriers did not see each other, due to the curvature of the earth).

However, when it came to the European theatre of World War II, very few knew more than Dunquerqe, El Alamain, D Day (all had seen the movie "The longest Day"), The Battle of the Bulge (also a movie) and Stalingrad. Thus, Hollywood was the principal teacher of history. And, according to Hollywood the English won the war practically singlehandedly. Of course I would bring up the other major battles: Moscow, Kursk and Khalkhin Gol.

Khalkhin Gol is very unique in the following way. The forces involved were rather small, as far as World War II was concerned especially for the Soviet Union. They were roughly the size of the Battle of the Bulge, less than 20 divisions on each side. (In fact, it is my humble opinion that any battle involving less than 5 divisions or 100,000 soldiers is not a battle but a "BRAWL." Therefore, in the entire history of Western Civilization England was never involved in a battle.)

The battle of Khalkhin Gol raged while Germany and the Soviet Union were negotiating the "10 YEAR NON AGGRESSION PACT." That is, just prior to the start of World War II. Just before the invasion of Poland. Up to that point, the Japanese army was invincible. They had conquered China, Korea and Manchuria. They set up an independent state of Manchukou (for Manchuria). Allied with Germany, they brought in German engineering to build defensive walls on their border. Then, convinced of their invincibility they began harassing the Soviets along a 30 mile stretch of that border. They were planning to invade Siberia and were looking for an "excuse." So, they invited all the European reporters who could make it, to witness their future stellar defeat of the Soviets.

Stalin had nobody to send to help the Soviet forces in Manchuria. So, he sent Grigori Zhukov (my uncle on my father's side). Zhukov reorganized the Soviet army and attacked the Japanese when they least expected it. He caught them in a huge pincer and wiped them out.

At first one might say, so what? What is so special about that? So, let me tell you what is so special about that. This defeat was a major blow to Japanese prestige. Up until that battle the ARMY had funding priority and directed the daily progress of the war in the Pacific. However, with that defeat priority, direction and funding shifted to the NAVY. And, the Japanese Navy just got a new commander: Isoroku Yamamoto. His strategy singled out America as the main enemy of Japan. Therefore, the American Navy had to be destroyed. His new target became PEARL HARBOR. Thus, the direction of the war changed in Japan from land to sea.

Of course, Zhukov gained fame and respect with Stalin and in the Soviet Union. He became a member of the STAVKA, the military council of war. In addition he had developed a new cadre of commanders that became indispensable in his succeeding victories at Stalingrad, Kursk and the capture of Berlin.

While Hitler looked at the dismal performance of the leaderless Soviet army which tried to defeat the tiny army of Finland, he should have looked at Khalkhin Gol. But then, "beauty lies in the eyes of the beholder."

Nowadays most western historians place Khalkhin Gol among the 40 most significant battles ever fought of all time. At par with Moscow, Stalingrad, Kursk and Midway!!!

(Example: see "The Decisive Battles of World History" by Professor Gregory S. Aldrete, University of Wisconsin Green Bay).

The 1000 Year War

You have heard of the 100 year war, have you not? And then there was the 30 year war, and the 10 year war, and the 7 year war, and the 6 year war, and the 5 year war, and of course there was the 6 day war. Well, let me add to this "heap of wars" the 1000 year war.

Let me show you that one entity, directed, encouraged, promoted, provided support and initiative to carry on that war. Of course that entity was the Papacy in Rome.

You have to keep in mind that "literacy" was reserved mostly for the clergy. Thus, practically all history books in Europe were written by the clergy, mostly Bishops or monks. They never had a mean word for the Pope or the Patriarch until the "Reformation." Even after the reformation very few historians were willing to antagonize the Pope or the Catholic Church.

However, in 1946 a "new Sheriff came to town" and decided to become the new "Gendarme of the World," the United States of America. Hopefully, nothing will be the same. So, let us begin with the history of the 1000 year war.

When the Papacy was created in 800 AD with the concordat between Charlemagne and the Patriarch of Rome. The weak link was the Papacy, even though Pope Leo III crowned Charlemagne. For the next 270 years the Emperor dominated the Pope. In fact the Papacy lived in fear of a reprisal from Constantinople or a whimsical removal by the Emperor and the replacement by an "ANTIPOPE." But, the Eastern Christian Empire was under attack from the Muslims and was in no position to respond. (At the same time Spain was under attack from the Moors.)

However, the first order of business for the Papacy was to "cement" the election of the Holy Roman Emperor. Since Western Europe was overrun by Goths, the Pope decided that they had to be kept out, because they were very tolerant of other faiths: Jews, Arian Christians, Monophysites and Orthodox Christians. (For example, the Merowingian Goths were called the "DO NOTHING KINGS" because they tolerated all religious minorities). Therefore, it was established that only "ELECTORS" could elect a Holy Roman Emperor. Thus, 4 Bishops and 3 Dukes were designated "FOREVER" (a hereditary title) to be the chosen electors. Since the Emperor created the Bishops and Dukes it was a "shoe in" for the ruling dynasty to stay in power. That is, the HOHENSTAUFFEN (in accordance with the German Concordat).

Start of the 1000 Year War: 946

936 In that year Otto I was crowned and anointed in Aachen (Charlemagne's capital) ushering in the beginning of the 1000 year war. His attendants were the Duke of Franconia (steward), the Duke of Swabia (cup bearer), the Duke of Lorraine (chamberlain), and the Duke of Bavaria (marshall).

951 to 952 Otto I invades Italy, but the Pope refuses to crown him Emperor, unless he defeats the Magyars.

955 Otto I, defeats the Magyars at Lechfeld (near Augsburg) and converts them to the Catholic faith.

961 to 964 Otto I invades Italy a second time, becomes King of Italy, is crowned at Pavia.

962 Otto I is crowned Emperor, after deposing one Pope and setting up another.

968 Otto I consolidates the Bishoprics of Brandenburg, Merseburg, Meissen and Zeits into the Bishopric of Magdeburg the future jump off point for the conquest of the East.

Thus, from 800 to 1073, the Emperor was the dominant force while the Papacy was subservient. Yet the Pope urged constantly the Emperor to create one Catholic Empire. However, in his eagerness to dominate the Christian Church, the Patriarch of Rome heaped all the prior titles of the Emperor of Rome on the new Emperor of the Holy Roman Empire (Charlemagne), including the title of Pontifex Maximus. This allowed the Emperor to designate or "invest" in Bishops.

However, a new wind started blowing in the monastery of Cluny in France. The groundwork was set to redefine the "mission" of the Papacy. It was formulated there that the Catholic Church was "CREATED by GOD." Hence, it was not subject to imperial power. Thus, in 1073 Pope Gregory VII (1073 to 1085) demanded the title PONTIFEX MAXIMUS back from the Emperor (Henry IV). Henry made a feeble attempt to combat Gregory. Henry assembled his loyal Bishops in Worms in 1076 and had them proclaim their independence from Gregory. But, Gregory fired back with his "heavy artillery." He excommunicated Henry and told the clergy and Bishops that they better not stay loyal to Henry. On January 25, 1077 Henry was seeking penance at Canossa, standing barefoot in the snow, dressed in sack cloths. Actually, the battle for the "INVESTITURE" was not over until 1122 (with the Concordat of Worms) at which time the Pope got the precious title and the Emperor got 5 Dukes instead of 3 as electors. Thus, the total number of electors went from 7 to 9.

The (External) Crusades

The feature and attraction of the Crusades was the fact that the Crusader was absolved of all wrong doings for a period of one year, or as long as he or she was on the Crusade. Thus, the Crusader was encouraged to steal, rape, plunder and destroy at will. Thus, while the "greater goal" was to liberate Jerusalem, the real objective was to plunder Asia Minor and bring that wealth to Western Europe. All you have to do is to follow the trail of promotions and the progress of the Crusades.

First, Asia Minor is plundered (Crusades 1 to 3), then Constantinople is plundered (Crusade 4). Now that the East has been thoroughly plundered a new slogan is formed: "The road to Jerusalem begins in

Cairo," which until that time had not been plundered. Thus, Crusades 5 to 7 are launched against Cairo but fail. When that fails, a new slogan is created: "The road to Jerusalem begins with Tunis, then Cairo." Thus, with each failure a new target is picked until Algeria, Morocco and Tunisia become the "Garden of France."

THE CRUSADES

External Crusades

1096 People's Crusade, led by Peter the Hermit.

1096 to 1099 First Crusade, takes Edessa, Antioch, Tripoli and Jerusalem. Plunders and devastates the Near East.

1147 to 1149 Second Crusade, dissention and failure. Still, the Near east is plundered and devastated.

1189 to 1192 Third Crusade, failure to capture Jerusalem. Little to plunder in the Near East.

1202 to 1204 Fourth Crusade, shift in target. Constantinople is sacked and plundered. Start of the RENAISSANCE as the plundered books are sold in ITALY.

1212 The Children Crusade. Nicholaus leads the German children and Stephan (a shepherd) leads the French children. The Children are captured by pirates and sold into slavery.

1218 to 1221 Fifth Crusade, a new target is set for plunder with the slogan: The road to Jerusalem begins with Cairo, Egypt. Crusaders are defeated.

1228 to 1229 Sixth or "Bloodless Crusaded." King Frederick II of South Italy negotiates possessions of Jerusalem, Bethlehem and Nazareth.

1248 to 1254 Seventh Crusade, led by King Louis IX against Cairo (target Jerusalem). Eventually his starving crusaders were ransomed for 800,000 pieces of gold.

1269 Aragonese Crusade. King James of Aragon launches crusade but is unable to land in Asia Minor, due to a storm.

1270   Eight Crusade. King Louis IX, instead of invading Cairo directly invades TUNIS. But, an epidemic killed many Crusaders including King Louis IX.

1365 to 1369 Crusade of Peter I of Cyprus. He captured and sacked Alexandria but was assassinated.

1396   Crusade of Nicopolis. Crusaders (mostly French) were defeated at Nicopolis (Bulgaria).

1443 to 1444 The Last Crusade. King Ladislas of Poland was soundly defeated at Varna by Murad II.

Internal Crusades

In addition to the external crusades, the Papacy directed and preached for INTERNAL crusades for about 300 years to eradicate all heresies. In particular against the Albigensiens, Cathars, Bogomils, Monophysites and Jews.

The difference between the two TYPES of CRUSADES were the DISPENSATIONS. For external crusades all dispensations were at least ONE YEAR. That is, the property and debts were frozen for the crusader and were protected by the POPE. This allowed the crusader to rape, murder, pillage as much as he wanted because he was "absolved" for all "transgressions."

For INTERNAL crusades the dispensations were only 30 days. Therefore any campaign lasted much longer, because it was very difficult to recruit enough knights for a campaign. For example:

1179 Third Lateran Council condemns Catharism and authorizes Crusades, which last about 300 years.

1208 to 1226 The Albigensian Crusade was one of many internal crusades.

1290 Jews are expelled from England.

1306 Jews are expelled from France.

1307 Knights Templars are suppressed in France.

Formation of ORDERS and KNIGHTS

When the crusading knights returned home from a crusade they were so used to "making war," that their energies had to be channeled into another "direction." Therefore, the Pope created "orders" and gave each order a "charter." Each order was led by a "Grandmaster," who was directly responsible to the Pope.

Hospitalers: were charged with the pilgrim's welfare on their pilgrimage to Jerusalem.

Templars: became the financiers who invented "letters of credit." They were formed by the Pope in 1128. Soon they were the richest and most powerful order. They became the envy of the indebted King of France. The King of France had their leaders arrested, tortured and executed as heretics (1307.) The remaining Templars vanished. The order was dissolved 1312 by the Synod of Vienne. Their property was transferred to the kings of France, Spain and the Hospitalers.

Teutonic Knights: The Teutonic Order was formed in 1156 with the mission to conquer the EAST (Heathens and Orthodox Christians alike). In 1226 they conquered the Prussians, a Slavic/Gothic people. They took their name and became the "landed nobility of the Germanic people," using the title:VON. In 1410 they were defeated by a coalition of Lithuanians, Poles and Ukrainians at Tannenberg (Grunwald when Polish). They had to sign a treaty limiting their expansion to the Vistula River. Thereupon the Grandmaster "ran to the Pope" and explained his dilemma. The Pope, however, saw no problem at all. He told the Grandmaster to transfer all his knights to a new order: THE KNIGHTS OF THE SWORD. Since this new order was not restricted to any treaty they could continue their conquest in the East. That order survived until 1840.

Free Companions: When the Crusaders returned to France in 1359 they promised to fight for France during the 100 year war. Since they were not paid for their services they plundered the countryside, so much so, that the King of France John "pawned them off" to Spain to fight the Saracens.

Jesuits: Formed in the 1530's and officially recognized by the Pope and Church in 1540. It was "chartered" to detect and fight any heresy by any means possible. The order grew from 10 to over 15,000 worldwide by the 17th century. The most "infamous" predecessor was Thomas de Torquemada (1420 to 1498). His reign of terror became legendary.

Knights of Columbus: They were created in the 17th century to combat the "Illuminati and Masons." President J.F. Kennedy was a Knight of Columbus.

1338 Edward III, the King of England claimed the French throne and the 100 year war began. The real origin of the 100 year war goes back to Richard I (1189 to 1199). When Richard decided to go on a crusade (Third Crusade) he left this two sons in the custody of his brother John. Besides being King of England, Richard ruled the greater part of France. While on the crusade, word came back to England that Richard had been killed. Thereupon, John killed both sons of Richard and proclaimed himself king (1199 to 1216).

The Pope decided to intervene since Richard was a Crusader.
The Pope called John to a conference to explain himself.
   But, John refused to go. The Pope slapped an INTERDICT on England and threatened to take away Richard's possessions outside of England. John goes and meets with the Pope.
   There, John gives away the English possessions on the continent except for Calais. While John is away, the English Barons write the "Magna Carta" and force John to sign it when he returns (1215). Thereupon, John sends a messenger to the Pope telling him that he had to sign the Magna Carta. The Pope issues a "Bull" telling the English Barons that whoever tried to enforce the Magna Carta would be excommunicated. Thus, the Pope and John started the 100 year war and the Magna Carta had no validity whatsoever until the reign of Elizabeth I.

   During the course of the 100 year war, the English won all the battles until Joan of Arc liberated Orleans (1429) and crowned the French King in Reims. Then, she became a "liability" to the French King. She was allowed to be captured by the Burgundians who turned her over to the English who burned her at the stake (1431).

(History repeats itself over and over again. Other examples: Caesar and Pompei, Hitler and Roehm, Stalin and Trotsky etc. Also, many French authors use the Burgundians as the villains in their plays. For example: Victor Hugo uses a Burgundian villain in "Rigoletto," in Verdi's opera).

1410 The Teutonic knights are defeated at Tannenberg (Grunwald) and are forced to sign a treaty whereby their expansion to the EAST was limited to the Vistula river. The GRANDMASTER of the TEUTONIC KNIGHTS went to ROME to see the Pope and described his dilemma. The Pope listened and then announced:

"This is not a problem. Take all your knights and we form a new order called "THE KNIGHTS of the SWORD, and continue your conquest of the EAST." This became the "STAIN" on German honor. Thus, when the Russians were defeated in the East by the Germans in World War I, it was called the Battle of Tannenberg in 1914. It "equalized" the defeat at Tannenberg of 1410. According to A.Solzhenitsin in his book called: August 1914. There, he claims the Russian Army, led by Samsonov was defeated by "Francois," a German general of French extraction. But, a battle so significant could not be credited to a "Frenchman." Therefore, von Hindenburg was transferred from the Western Front to the Eastern Front to take credit for this "EPIC VICTORY."

Knights of the Sword: Created in 1410 to replace the Teutonic Knights. The order survived until 1840.

1494 Treaty of Tordesillas, a town in the Azores. In 1492 Christopher Columbus discovered America. Following that discovery the Pope, Alexander VI and the Emperor, Maximillian met hastily to outline an orderly conquest and plunder of the newly found lands and people. The East was given to Portugal while the West was given to Spain, depriving all other European nations in this worldwide plunder. Each "CONQUISTADOR" was assigned a priest who was the representative of the Pope and guided the conquerors in their actions. (It should be noted that Stalin was a seminary student and used that method to control his military commanders by assigning

"COMMISSARS," who had the final word as to what was in line with the party's ideology and what was not).

1509 to 1547 Henry VIII, King of England. Much ado is made of Henry's attempt to divorce Katherine of Aragon and marry Ann Boylin. (Many Kings before and after got the desired divorces when they paid the "right" fee to the Pope).

Example: Hedwig and Jagellon. The real reason Henry breaks with the Catholic Church and the Pope is because England is EXCLUDED from plundering the newly discovered lands. Thus, in 1534 Henry is excommunicated when he establishes the Church of England. This deprives the Pope of the REVENUE and CONTROL (Clergy). But Henry does not break with the Holy Roman Empire paying his annual tribute to the Emperor. Thus, by dividing loyalties, Henry stays "friendly" with the Emperor. Henry is succeeded by 10 year old Edward VI (1547 to 1453), then by Mary (1553 to 1558) who restores the Catholic Church. In 1554, Mary marries Philip of Spain. But then Elizabeth I, becomes Queen of England (1558 to 1603).

When she restores the Anglican Church, Elizabeth is excommunicated (1570) and the Pope places a bounty of 2 million Ducats on the reconquest of England. That bounty is in effect to this day. It has never been lifted. Over time many rulers tried to collect that bounty. For example:

Philip of Spain with the Spanish Armada in 1588.

Napoleon planned to invade and collect the bounty but was defeated by English pirates and regulars at Trafalgar in 1805. (Thus, to raise capital, he sold the French colonies in America!) Hitler planned to collect the bounty in his 6 year war 1939 to 1945, aka: World War II. But, when Goering could not defeat the English Air Force, Hitler opted for invading the Soviet Union instead, and earn the "batan," for the survival of the 1000 year REICH.

Conquest of the Americas: When the natives rebelled to the plunder and genocide by the Conquistadors and the Clergy, they were massacred mercilessly (even though many western historians call these massacres battles).

1521 Tenochtitian, the Aztecs were massacred.

1532 Cajamarca, the Inca were massacred.

It should be noted that incredible wealth was plundered from the American natives and transferred to Spain. Emperor Philip II became the "RICHEST PERSON" in Europe. Yet within ONE GENERATION that wealth was wasted on petty wars and left Spain bankrupt. Therefore, beware playing the "Gendarme of the World."

1571 Lepanto: The Pope preached a "naval crusade" against the Muslims. Spain, Venice and Austria combined and defeated the Muslims at Lepanto, ending their mediterranean threat.

1572 St.Bartholomew massacre: The Pope, Catherine de Medici and Charles Duke of Guise (1525 to 1574) was Cardinal Archbishop of Rheims conspired to massacre the French Protestants (Huguenots), as they attended a wedding.

1618 to 1648 The 30 Year War. When we speak of the "Reformation," we generally speak of Martin Luther and 1517 when he nailed his 95 Thesis on the door of his church against the abuses of the Catholic Church and the Pope. However, there were reformers at least 40 years before that date, for example: Girolamo Savonaola (1452 to 1498) and others. The Papacy was slow in responding and by 1618 nearly half of Western Europe was Protestant. Then, the Pope preached for a "COUNTER REFORMATION" to restore the Catholic Church. Thus, from 1618 and until 1648 religious wars raged mostly in central Europe until it was utterly devastated. Toward the end, Sweden saved the Reformation. Finally, the Treaty of Westphalia set the religious tone by letting the RULER determine the religion.

1683 The Ottoman Turks decided to conquer all of Western Europe. They assembled a huge army (300,000 strong) and launched their invasion. But, in their way was Vienna, a fortified city which had to be taken. As soon as the Muslims launched their offensive, the Pope began preaching a crusade against them and for volunteers to help defend Vienna. But, at that time all western powers were waging wars against each other. The only response came from the Polish King John III Sobieski and the Ukrainian Cossacks who were the only ones who knew how to fight the Janissaries. They came to Vienna and liberated Vienna. But, when they asked for water and hay for their horses (which was in abundance in Vienna) they were not allowed admittance and were given no water and no hay. (Goes to show you that: NO GOOD DEED GOES UNPUNISHED.)

1804 to 1814 Napoleon I, Emperor: The French Revolution was against the Nobility, the Clerics and the Pope. In fact at the height of the revolution a local prostitute was installed in Notre Dame as the "GODDESS OF REASON."

As Napoleon grew stronger in Europe he "restored" the Pope (1801 concordat) to have himself crowned Emperor (1804).

Yet Napoleon crowned himself.

After the Battle of Jena (1806) he met the beautiful and 17 year old Maria Walevska who was madly in love with him. They had an affair and Napoleon got her pregnant. (She was a Polish patriot and she saw Napoleon as the salvation for Poland). This raised Napoleons expectations a few notches.

Now, Napoleon wanted to create a "DYNASTY." (All this time he thought he was impotent since Josephine produced no children).

So, he divorced Josephine, resurrected the Hapsburgs and married Marry Louise, a Hapsburg (1809). Then he wanted to take over the "batan" from the Hapsburgs as the protector of the Pope (to solidify his dynasty). The Pope was more than willing to give him the "batan," provided he conquered Russia and converted them to the Roman Faith. Thus, from then on Napoleon's wars were "HOLY WARS."

1914 to 1918 World War I: When the Archduke of Austria was assassinated in SARAJEVO, Austria demanded that all guilty parties be released to Austrian Authorities, this was done with the consent of Germany and the Pope. Serbia felt threatened and appealed to Russia, who promised them aid and began mobilizing. Thereupon Germany gave Russia an ULTIMATUM which was impossible to comply with, even if Russia did her utmost. Now the "chain of alliances" kicked in. France had to support Russia and England had to support France. Thus, the "WAR to END all Wars" started.

1939 to 1945 World Was II: When Adolph Hitler began his campaign in earnest to put the National Socialist Party in power he had to secure the Catholic vote. Thus, he made a concordat with the Pope putting the Catholics into a privileged position starting in 1933. After Hitler defeated France, he had intentions to collect the 2 million Ducat bounty set on the conquest of England (Operation Sea Lion). But, when Goering failed to destroy the RAF, Hitler made a new concordat with the Pope to conquer the Soviet Union. This would give him the "BATAN" as the new protector of the POPE (replacing the Austrians) which he deemed essential for the survival of the 1000 year Reich. Thus, the new slogan became: THE CONQUEST OF ENGLAND IS THROUGH THE CONQUEST OF THE SOVIET UNION. (Does it have a familiar ring?[Crusades])

1946 Nuremberg Trial: The top twenty Nazi hoodlums were tried, but in the process the Pope and the Catholic Church were implicated as collaborators of the Third Reich in the Holocaust. In particular as countless high ranking Nazis bought themselves passage to South America as members of a Bishop's entourage.

The 1000 year war ends with the Trial at Nuremberg. Thus the entire span was about 1000 years, or from 935 to 1946

It should be noted that wars have accomplished very little in the long run. They have created nothing but poverty to the conquering nation. For example: Philip II, was the "richest man in Europe" (with all that plunder from the Americas). Yet within his lifetime he wasted all that wealth on petty wars, leaving Spain bankrupt at his death. Another good example is Louis XIV, the "Sun King" of France. He wasted the wealth of France on petty wars which left France poor and bankrupt, leading to the French Revolution. Instead, DIPLOMACY should be used as much as possible and leave armed conflict only as a last resort! For example: Frederick II, accomplished more with diplomacy than all the Crusades combined.

Today there is a new "SHERIFF in town": The United States of America. Of course if you read American History you might think that starting with World War II, we won every war. But, the reality is far from the truth. Yes, we defeated Japan; but, we have not won a war since (Korea, Vietnam, Iraq, Afganistan and so on). Except for countries like Panama and Grenada we have not won a single conflict. While we claim to have defeated the Nazis, a closer look reveals that we "SAVED FRANCE" from falling into the sphere of Soviet control. Modern Historians reveal that not a single allied battle in Europe was decisive. Not D Day, not Bastogne and not Remagen. We could have accomplished all this without losing a single soldier through diplomacy. (Gregory S. Aldrete published "The Decisive Battles of World History." According to him, the only decisive battles of World War II were: 1939 Khalkhin Gol, 1942 Midway and 1942 Stalingrad). Other historians include Moscow and Kursk.

Playing the "Gendarme" of the world is expensive (in terms of money), costly (in terms of human life) and often counter productive (we often accomplish just the opposite). For the next 100 years we will be facing a determined and formidable foe: The Muslims. Their target is actually Israel. However, practically every "ISLAMIC REPUBLIC" issues a stamp as a sign of solidarity, which depicts Israel with a knife stuck in it, and blood dripping from the blade.

However, they have learned that in order to defeat Israel, the United States must be defeated. Why? The United States is considered to be a Jewish State. Why?

1) Of the 5,000 religions in the United States only seven (Catholic, Orthodox, Lutheran, Anglican, Muslim, Hindu and Buddhism) are generally recognized religions. Most others are considered to be "Jewish Sects."

2) Practically all "TELEVANGELISTS" read from the "Old Testament," hence they preach "Jewish" history.

3) Practically all males in the United States are circumcised, a Jewish and Muslim custom.

4) The United States is run by the Masons, at the very top it is heavily Jewish.

5) Many Senators and Representatives are Jewish and have dual citizenship, a disproportionate number when compared to the population.

6) In 1960 the Jews have been absolved by the Pope of killing Jesus Christ.

Traditionally, the Jews had one safe haven when they were persecuted by Christians, they were sheltered by the Muslims. But, these days are over, ever since the State of Israel was created in 1948 and the Palestinians were evicted.

One last thought. The rule of 72 gives us a good measure to estimate the "doubling" process. Today the Muslim World is 1.8 billion strong. It grows at a rate of 6.5% annually. That means it doubles about every 11 years. This means that in 100 years the Muslim population will be about 500 billion strong, while the rest of the world population will remain about the same or at most double. Thus, in the "worst case scenario" there will be 500 billion Muslims competing against 8 billion non Muslims for resources. Let's hope that technology will provide us with an answer.

Let us take one last look at the 1000 year war. The External Crusades lasted about 350 years (1096 to 1444); the Internal crusades lasted about 300 years; the plunder of the Americas lasted about 350 years (1494 to 1850); the plunder of the EAST with the Teutonic Knights and the Knights of the Sword lasted nearly 700 years (1156 to 1840); the Inquisition lasted about 400 years; the Counter Reformation lasted about 150 years and in between were many isolated and prolonged wars, all directed and orchestrated by the Papacy in Rome!

Therefore, does it not make sense to have robbers steal from the plunderers? Of course it does. This is how we can look at the English pirates, who raided the Spanish galleons, which were bringing home the loot! However, does it justify piracy in the first place?